Governments Get It Wrong

Dennis C. Grube is a professor in politics and public policy at the University of Cambridge, and Acting Director of the Bennett Institute for Public Policy. A one-time political speechwriter in his native Tasmania, he is the author of three single-author monographs on aspects of politics and policy. *Why Governments Get It Wrong* is Grube's first book for a wide audience.

Why Governments Get It Wrong

And How They Can Get It Right

DENNIS C. GRUBE

PAN BOOKS

First published 2022 by Macmillan

This edition first published with a new preface 2023 by Pan Books
an imprint of Pan Macmillan
The Smithson, 6 Briset Street, London EC1M 5NR
EU representative: Macmillan Publishers Ireland Ltd, 1st Floor,
The Liffey Trust Centre, 117–126 Sheriff Street Upper,
Dublin 1, D01 YC43
Associated companies throughout the world
www.panmacmillan.com

ISBN 978-1-5290-8333-0

3 5 7 9 8 6 4

A CIP catalogue record for this book is available from the British Library.

Typeset by Palimpsest Book Production Ltd, Falkirk, Stirlingshire
Printed and bound by CPI Group (UK) Ltd, Croydon, CR0 4YY

Contents

Contents

Preface to the Paperback Edition

People in a hurry break things.

In politics, frenetic pace is often celebrated. It suggests enthusiasm, 'grip', and a determination not to be held back by the entrenched rules of the game. Every incoming government or presidential administration has a well-publicized plan for its first one hundred days. Individual politicians and officials work on even shorter timeframes. Who can forget the ten-day whirlwind of Anthony Scaramucci's reign as Director of Communications in the Trump White House? His memorable determination to be a transparent operator – a 'front-stabber' – may seem honourable in the clandestine world of political skulduggery, but it turns out that it can just as easily lead to chaos. Running fast with scissors is dangerous.

On 6 September 2022, Liz Truss was sworn in as Prime Minister of the United Kingdom. Less than two months later, she was gone. In the three hundred years or so since Robert Walpole's reign as the first recognized prime minister, none has enjoyed a shorter tenure in the role than Truss. In her case, the leadership campaign lasted longer than the leadership itself. Much has already been written by those journalists and political commentators who were tasked with diagnosing the malaise in real time. But the question still remains: how could an experienced, resolute political operator possess the skills to spend years climbing to the apex of British politics and yet prove so inept at staying in post?

Nobody could say that Truss, and the Chancellor with whom her fate was inextricably linked – Kwasi Kwarteng – had not prepared themselves for office. No one could say that they were policy free zones or wet-behind-the-ears newbies. They had been writing and thinking about politics together for over a decade as MPs. That now infamous volume, *Britannia Unchained*, had set out in 2012 the thoughts of a new generation of Conservative MPs, intent on radical reforms in the Thatcherite mould. Truss and Kwarteng had since sat around the cabinet table under multiple prime ministers and seen how the machinery of government works. They were relentlessly clear about the underpinning values and beliefs that supported their political views. They were in favour of smaller government, lower taxes, and a Britain that embraced innovation and growth. This was no hidden agenda. Truss talked about it for weeks on end as she toured the country during the leadership debates against Rishi Sunak. Conservative Party members watched on and liked what they heard. For Truss and Kwarteng, after years of pushing for their preferred political approach, their moment was now at hand. Their time had come. And there was no time to lose.

But people in a hurry break things.

What I set out in this book is a list of four elements that governments need to consider to even have a chance of winning the politics of public policy. They are not a guarantee of success, but a suggestion on where to start looking when things feel like they're going wrong. The possibility of success is predicated on four aspects – the four 'ducks' that must find their way into a row. There must be a clearly defined problem; an understandable story about why it's a problem; some convincing data and evidence to back that up; and the right policy solution. Many politicians know these things instinctively. They are the core ingredients of what we might call political savvy, or street-smarts.

But, as most of us know from our own lives, in moments of stress or panic we can forget the fundamentals. In the morning rush, when there are a hundred things calling for our attention, we can charge out of the front door without our keys. We then pat our pockets and realize we left the mobile phone behind as well. But we have to get to work, so we charge on rather than stopping and systematically working out how we can rectify these problems.

That, in a nutshell, is what happened to the Truss government. It ran out of the house and just kept running. The knowledge that there were only two years to go until the next election ensured the stress. There was simply no time to stop and think. After a decade of talking about change, now was the time for action. Never mind that the country was exhausted after just having been through two years of pandemic nightmares. Never mind that the British economy was in a precarious state, with record-high government debt and the sudden economic shocks wrought by the outbreak of war in Ukraine. This context simply had to be ignored if this unique moment was to be fully seized. Truss and Kwarteng's time had come.

So the charge began towards what was surely the most momentous mini-budget in British history. The ducks were not just out of alignment, they were barely in the same pond. Policies landed like artefacts from the blue, emerging into view without the context needed to make sense of them. Take the policy to lift the cap on bankers' bonuses in the City of London, floated to the press by the Chancellor soon after taking office. Kwasi Kwarteng is nobody's fool. A former Kennedy Scholar at Harvard, with a Ph.D. in economic history from Cambridge – and even a *University Challenge* quiz show winner's trophy – he was rightly seen as someone with the intellectual tools required for the job at hand.

What was missing was the story on why this bankers' cap had to go. Nobody had taken the time to really shape the problem and explain it to the public in a way that would make sense to people on ordinary incomes, who were watching their own earnings being eaten away by 10 per cent inflation. Why was this the most urgent priority? There may well, in fact, be a good policy story to be told about the City of London driving the British economy. There may in fact be solid evidence that bankers were looking favourably at New York or Hong Kong because of the cap on their earnings in London. And removing the cap may actually be the right policy response if we want this problem fixed.

It was impossible to know for sure, because there was no well-defined problem. There was no captivating story about change being vital. There was no concrete evidence on the economic and social costs to Britain of keeping that cap on bonuses in place. All the public were given was the policy itself, dropped at their feet whilst the government ran past them, scissors in hand, ready to dispatch the next burden to the British economy.

As the mini-budget revealed just one week later, the next ribbon to cut was the 45 per cent top rate of income tax. Here was another measure wholly consistent with the Truss and Kwarteng world view. They had for many years been saying that they believed cutting taxes was the best way to ensure economic growth. What shocked was the determination to start that journey with the top rate of tax. In the absence of a better story, the narrative that took hold was that the Truss government made life easier for those who already had it easy. That is undoubtedly an unfair characterization of what Truss and Kwarteng felt they were trying to do, but their own rationale was unclear. Again, there was no strong sense that the highest tax rate was in itself a policy problem that needed immediate resolution. The evidence of the impact of that rate as a drag on growth or innovation was scarce. The Office for Budget Responsibility was denied the chance to provide evidence and modelling of its own. Once more, all the public got was the policy itself, a piece of economic flotsam drifting past the eyeline of a confused and wary populace.

The rest, as they say, is history. So disastrous was the fallout from the mini-budget that the Truss government never recovered. The prime minister sacrificed first the policies – reversing almost the entirety of the mini-budget – and then the Chancellor himself, but to no avail. After a total of forty-four days in office, Prime Minister Truss announced her resignation outside the iconic door of Number 10, defiantly listing her achievements and lamenting that she could not 'deliver the mandate on which she was elected by the Conservative Party'. A tumultuous end to an extraordinary government.

It will be for future historians to make full sense of these astonishing events. As ever, the whole story is infinitely more complex and complicated than a few policies being poorly received. My goal here is simply to make the point that having a good policy idea is, in itself, never enough. That idea needs to be a response to a specific problem that people can understand. It needs to be supported by evidence, data, and independent analysis. And it needs to be situated within a story; a narrative to make sense of it beyond the generalities of 'supporting economic growth' or 'building a stronger society'.

That is the lesson of the Truss experience. And it is not limited to the UK, or to any particular side of politics. As I outline in the pages that follow, it is a lesson that applies equally at all levels. From local mayors regulating the keeping of animals, to presidents contemplating wars, the fundamentals of the four ducks are the same. I offer examples from left and right, big countries and small, to show how governments go wrong as they wrestle with the challenges of policymaking.

It is perhaps time that the old adage of 'a week is a long time in politics' was retired. It doesn't seem to do justice to the true freneticism that can at times grip our modern debates. An hour is a long time in politics now. Amidst the sense of never-ending crisis, and the desire to move at speed, it is easy to forget that politics does have some fundamental rules at play. And that it is still possible to get those four ducks to align at short notice. But it only happens when you take the time to feed them, to coax them into line, and start them swimming. Then governments earn their ticket at the starting gate of policymaking. It can be done quickly, but not in a mad panic.

Because people in a hurry break things.

Why
Governments
Get It
Wrong

Prologue

Some readers will remember a fabulous song from the early 2000s by Natasha Bedingfield. It's called 'These Words'. It is literally a song about writing a song. It's about scratching your head, throwing some lines on a page, and hoping like hell that they connect together. Ripping up that page and starting again. Giving in to despair momentarily and staring into the abyss, before suddenly finding the story you want to tell.

For a few fascinating years in the late 2000s, I was a political speechwriter in the Australian state of Tasmania. I too was often ripping up sheets of paper as the words refused to gel. Staring into the abyss was a daily exercise. Great phrases would run through my head as I dashed around the corridors, the words buttressed only by delusions of my own self-importance. Sometimes I'd listen to great speeches on YouTube in the background, just to get in the zone when I was writing. Obama's victory night speech in 2008; Reagan at the Berlin Wall in 1987. How could one go wrong?

Well, you'd be surprised. Cascades of alliterative nonsense could be summoned up at will, but classic sentences were harder to find. It's difficult to sieve the wheat from the chaff when all you have is chaff. Small bursts of humour that looked good on the page could dissipate into vapour when delivered in the flesh. My words could deflate a room on a whim. I had the gift.

Fellow advisers would console me with typical Australian *sangfroid*. 'You can't polish a turd,' one used to say. They meant that if the policy or the political situation is bad enough, then it isn't the words used to describe it that are the problem. Now that I think about it, they might have meant that my speeches *were* the turd. That thought will fester.

But there were also wonderful moments. The extraordinary feeling when the words you've reached for do some justice to the topic at hand. When they connect. When you watch an audience nod along because you've captured a sentiment that means something to them. Those are the moments when words stop sounding like political babble and start to feel like something more real.

The truth, of course, is that these weren't my words at all. The only time they came out of my mouth was when I practised them at my desk. The true owners of the words were the people tasked with delivering them. I've seen politicians turn a flat speech into a joyous one by changing 'my' words on their feet. It's part instinct, part skill, and impressive to watch. Politicians get a lot of bad press all around the world. And so they should. Democracy is not here to mollycoddle its rulers. But too often that also masks the reality that they are doing unbelievably complex jobs with a skill and a passion that would surprise you. I sat with my pen in the shadows, whilst far more courageous people took the products of that pen out into the spotlight. It was they who took responsibility for the words they shared with the world. I admired them immensely for it.

But the words also had a wider importance. What politicians say defines who they are. It shapes a government's policy agenda. The words we use to describe a problem go on to influence the story – the narrative – on what the government should do about that problem. Despite the much-debated merits of 'spin', even good words can't do much to save a bad policy. They sure don't help much if the evidence isn't there to support the message, or if the purported policy solution on offer doesn't match the complexity of the issues involved. I reflected only little on these things during my time working in politics but have now spent over a decade thinking about them from the relative distance of academia.

This book is the result. It's intended for everyone who has ever sat in front of the nightly news with a mixture of puzzlement and rage. 'Why is the government doing this?', you ask as you gesticulate at the TV with waving arms. This book provides some insights into what the government is at least *trying* to do. It also highlights how easily these apparently simple things turn to dust with depressing regularity. In essence, the government is trying to identify what's wrong, work out *why* it's wrong, explain the problem to the public, and decide what they're going to do to fix it. How hard can that be?

It's a lot tougher than it looks.

Introduction – The Four Ducks

Britain gets cold in December. The days get short and dark. Sometimes the simple glow of the TV seems to offer warmth. Even the sight of a smiling news anchor can feel like a welcome connection to the outside world. In December 2019, viewers tuning in across Britain saw an election campaign in full flight. Flashing images offered glimpses of our politicians at work, fighting for votes. And what better way to fight for votes than through the age-old medium of a campaign stunt.

We are used to seeing British prime ministers standing outside 10 Downing Street at a lectern. We are used to seeing them standing at the despatch box in Parliament, jousting with the opposition. We are even used to seeing them out and about in the street, shaking hands with constituents and listening to their concerns. What we are not used to is seeing them in charge of construction machinery. Prime Minister Boris Johnson decided this had to change.

The single most dominant issue of the 2019 UK election was Brexit. For four long years, the very word had been inserted into every political conversation. Since the referendum of 2016, when the British people voted by a small majority to leave the EU, there was simply no other game in town. Brexit sucked the political oxygen out of every other aspect of public life. By 2019, there was an immense weariness creeping in. Even politicians and journalists looked as if they'd had enough. Every parliamentary vote, every policy announcement, every political defection was viewed solely through the lens of Brexit. How on earth could the UK finally get rid of this issue? How could it metaphorically break through to the other side?

To break through things, you need a tool to give you some leverage. A hammer can break through small obstructions. A crowbar can prise open a door. A chainsaw can carve down a troublesome tree. But what if the obstacle is bigger? What if it looms like a wall in front of you and every tool in your arsenal has so far bounced off? In cases like that, you need some serious kit. You need a howitzer capable of blasting apart that wall. Or, better yet, someone willing to drive a bulldozer right through it.

On 10 December, that's exactly what Boris Johnson did. The TV images that night showed an enormous wall of bricks (polystyrene bricks, but let's not quibble) representing the congestion that had descended upon the Brexit debate. To dial down any danger of nuance, the word 'GRIDLOCK' was emblazoned across the front of this barricade. In a burst of action, this wall was reduced to rubble, literally bulldozed out of the way in front of our eyes. As the metaphorical dust was clearing, viewers strained to see who had dealt so imperiously with this once impregnable wall of Brexit confusion. They soon discerned, rising triumphantly from his machine, the figure of their prime minister.

This was the single most effective image of the whole campaign. The fact that it was simultaneously also the single most absurd image of the whole campaign didn't matter. The image did exactly what it was supposed to do. It turned a complex policy reality into a very simple story. And the hero of that story knew how to cut through this debate: with a digger. All that was missing was a hard hat.

Hard hats and high-vis vests: these are the foundation items in every politician's wardrobe. They invariably look terrible when actually worn, clinging inauthentically to their wearer. There is something strangely incongruous about a fluorescent vest worn over a well-pressed suit. And those hats never seem to quite fit, remaining perched on top of the head without a firm anchor. But politicians love them because they are garments of action. In a visual age they are a signifier that this is a person who is willing to get stuck in on behalf of their people. It's a way of bringing a policy decision to life so that the voters can see that something is actually happening.

The garments are necessary because public policy has a perception problem. Public policy sounds boring. It sounds elitist. It sounds removed from the everyday issues that normal people have to struggle with. The irony, of course, is that the opposite is true. Policy is how we change the world.

Policy is what governments do. Deciding whether or not to renew nuclear weapons is a policy decision. The provision of an old-age pension, the setting of higher-education fees, or the availability of vaccines for infants – these are all public policy decisions. From starting a war, to determining how often rubbish bins should be collected, public policy touches every aspect of life in every country on earth. We entrust our governments to make decisions on all these things.

The problem is that governments muck things up. All the

time. From potholes that never seem to disappear in our local street, to entire hospital systems that never seem to function smoothly. In America in 2020, economic stimulus cheques were allegedly sent to over a million dead people. Bad things happen.

But there is an alternative story too. These same governments sometimes do extraordinary things. In 1998, the Blair government in the UK, along with the people and politicians of Northern Ireland, and the governments of Ireland and the USA, worked together to bring the Good Friday Agreement into being. Decades of strife and centuries of distrust were pushed aside in an act of collective political will. In Finland, the determination of successive governments to improve education through the comprehensive school system saw this small Nordic nation dominate international education rankings for much of the early twenty-first century.[1]

What is the difference between these successes, and the failures that constantly surround us? This book will argue that success happens when governments get their ducks in a row. That means getting some fundamentals right to ensure they at least have a chance of winning at the politics of policy-making. To highlight what those ducks are, and how they work, let me start with an example where that didn't happen to see how this looks in practice.

We all remember our schooldays. For better or worse, they are formative. First cigarettes, first kisses, first fights. Great friends made and then lost. Teachers who terrify and those who inspire. Success and failure, fear and triumph – all endured with one eye towards the future. In most education systems around the world, these years ratchet up to some watershed moments that decide whether our schooling can take us where we want to go. In the English education system, this pinnacle arrives in the form of the exams known as the A-levels. It is these exams that determine whether or not students will get a university place.

Many readers will remember having to undergo exams at some point. It is frightening. Your hand shakes as you try and produce essays at such a speed that the writing becomes illegible. The names of monarchs, the clauses of the Magna Carta, and the cosine of x in an unintelligible equation jostle for space in students' brains. This is the system we have. Its single redeeming feature is that it works in delivering a sorting function. It constructs a hurdle that must be jumped. It categorizes student ability in a pitiless, merciless, heartbreaking process of narrowly based judgement. And that's just when things are going well.

But what happens if – one year – students are not able to sit those exams? The Covid pandemic crisis provided an answer. As the disease gathered pace across Europe in March 2020, decision-makers started to embrace the need for radical action. In the face of burgeoning transmission rates, overwhelming hospital admissions and increasingly frightening numbers of deaths each day, governments had to respond. In the UK, as in most European countries, lockdown followed. People were told to stay at home wherever possible. Economic activity was deliberately placed on hold to arrest the spread of the virus. All parts of life suffered, including the education system. In Britain, schools were closed, and students were sent home. Most importantly for our story, the fateful decision was taken not to hold those final exams. It was considered simply too dangerous to enclose thousands of students in small spaces to write answers to questions they had not even been able to study properly due to school closures.

How then could one decide between the competing academic merits of various students? In an education system that is built on marks, on competitive grading, the idea that the UK could simply have a gap year from exams had consequences. Most clearly, it meant universities would lose the normal means by which to judge whether students should be admitted or not. An answer had to be found.

The body which regulates exams and results in England is called the Office of Qualifications and Examinations Regulation, or Ofqual for short. Those who still think the Civil Service offers some kind of gravy-train livelihood should consider the experiences of the good folk at Ofqual. For them, 2020 was one hell of a rough year. As subsequently noted by Ofqual chair Roger Taylor in his evidence to a parliamentary committee, the regulator had a series of three preferences for how to handle this emergency. The first was to have the exams go ahead, despite the dangers of the Covid situation. The second – if the first was not considered possible – was to postpone the exams until conditions would allow them to take place. The third option was to go for a hybrid system, under which teachers' own assessments of their students would be mixed with statistical data in an algorithm to produce the grades. Ministers decided to plump for the third option.

But there were already some straws in the wind suggesting things might not go smoothly. In Britain, education is a 'devolved' policy area, meaning the constituent nations each run their own education system independently of each other. Wales, Scotland, Northern Ireland and England must each make their own decisions. Only two days before the English A-level results were to be announced, the Scottish government had performed a head-spinning policy U-turn. They had originally used the same policy approach as England, embracing the same combination of teacher assessments mixed with an algorithm, supported by the expertise of the Scottish Qualifications Authority. The algorithm was designed to use the previous results of schools as an indicator to moderate any over-grading of current students by excessively enthusiastic teachers.

The result was that around a quarter of Scottish students saw their predicted grades downgraded. What is more, the data showed that deprived areas were hit the hardest. If a student happened to be at a school that was not normally expected to do particularly well, they were more likely to have their marks reduced by the algorithm. The Scottish government found itself assailed by students, parents, and the press. In the face of the fiasco, they had no choice but to simply banish the algorithm altogether. The teachers' predicted grades for their students were accepted as the final grades. The resultant grade inflation was grudgingly embraced as an unavoidable side-effect of Covid-19.

The UK government looked north to Scotland with concern but decided to stick to its guns for the English results. They adopted a tone of reassurance. 'The system we have built for establishing grades is robust, fair and protects the interests of students,' wrote the Secretary of State for Education, Gavin Williamson, in the *Daily Telegraph* on 13 August 2020. This was the day that hundreds of thousands of students were receiving their A-level results. Students in England were encouraged to remain confident that everything was in good hands.

Then it all went horribly wrong. As it had in Scotland, it turned out that this 'robust and fair' system in fact downgraded many students' results, and in particular did so for those from the most deprived areas. The story the government was telling didn't seem to match the lived reality on the ground, as pictures of confused and angry students began to crowd on to TV news bulletins. Within days, the government was forced into a dramatic shift, as it too abandoned the algorithm altogether. The reprieve came too late for some students who had already lost their university place in the interim. The press had a field day. Words like 'fiasco' and 'shambles' leapt off the front pages amidst the mayhem. Calls for the Education Secretary Gavin Williamson to resign abounded. How had it come to this?

There are four elements that need to line up for governments to have a decent shot at winning the politics of policymaking in any given situation. These are the four ducks that have to end up in a row. They do not necessarily guarantee success, as interference from what we might call 'intervening variables' can still derail an otherwise successful policy process. Equally, politicians can sometimes just get lucky and have a policy success without aligning all four items. But look at the politics of most policy disasters and you'll find at least one of these four things is out of whack with the rest. Equally, unpack a policy success and you'll see these four items at its heart.

The first duck is what policy analysts call 'problem definition'. What is the actual problem that this policy is trying to solve? It sounds like a pretty straightforward question, but the answer comes preloaded with all kinds of difficulties. Problem definition is a combination of ideological worldview mixed with imperfect evidence, and then served up as urgent political action. It is subjective choice masquerading as objective analysis. Problem definition provides the frame of action for all that follows. What makes it difficult is that problem definition is a contest between competing views of that problem. Those views don't stand still, and neither does the problem. What begins as one issue can morph into another.

Take drug use by young people as an example. Is it a health problem, a social problem, or a law-and-order problem? It could in fact be all three. But how you define it shapes the playing field for what governments should reasonably do about it. That continues, even as the definitional questions become more specific. If it's a law-and-order problem, what is at its heart? Is it that drugs are too cheap and easily available? Is it that organized crime recruits dislocated young people? Each question defines the problem a little more. The reason it matters is that the problem definition determines whether a particular policy intervention has any chance of working. It provides the frame through which success or failure will be judged. Law-and-order advocates will say that setting up a needle exchange programme just encourages young people to inject drugs. It doesn't 'solve' the problem, as they see it. In contrast, health policy advocates will say that as young people are likely to take drugs anyway, this is the best way to keep them healthy while they're doing it.

But before we get to the policy itself, the next part of the puzzle is the choice of a narrative for action. This is where the ingredients of the problem definition are turned into a story. That story – or the policy 'narrative' – is the second duck that needs to come into alignment. The story has to be consistent with the problem definition and help to explain that problem in a way that connects with people. Any narrative is by definition a selective thing. Nobody ever tells the 'whole story' about anything, and government is no different. It seizes on particular facts and insights, and then sets out a story around them to explain why they are doing what they're doing.

To continue with the drug-use example, politicians employing a law-and-order problem definition will set out their narrative in a way that underpins their view of things. So they might tell a story about a young person who was sent to prison for drug use and turned their life around because of that intervention. Their narrative will highlight the successes that allegedly flow from zero-tolerance approaches. It's a story about self-discipline being built as a result of clear social boundaries and high expectations. The complex life challenges that might lead people to use drugs will be downplayed in favour of praising the strength of those who have been able to pick themselves up by their bootstraps.

Ultimately, any problem definition, and the narrative that accompanies it, will at some point have to deal with the facts of what is actually happening on the ground. The data and evidence are the third duck that must join this conga line towards policy success. At one level it is tempting to think that clear evidence will show up false narratives and faulty problem definitions as fraudulent. For two decades now, governments have talked about the benefits of 'evidence-based policy'. Phrases like 'data-driven' and 'led by the science' have become tropes that politicians use to present themselves as making rational choices. The truth is, of course, that evidence is never totally objective. Data do not speak for themselves, and 'science' is not always definitive. Scientists and social scientists know this all too well, but politics struggles when confronted by such ambiguity.

In most cases, the evidence itself is inconclusive. What you see depends on where you look. Those who see drug use as a symptom of permissive social boundaries would view the evidence on zero-tolerance policies in a favourable light. The now famous law-and-order approach to crime in New York in the 1990s, under Mayor Giuliani, was unmistakably successful in 'cleaning up' the streets. The data and evidence from multiple studies suggests that the aggressive policy approach worked. That is to say, it worked if the 'problem' was the need to stop minor illegality on the streets. Those who saw the problem as one of social and economic disadvantage view that same data and evidence very differently: they see an over-incarceration of already marginalized groups in an attempt to sweep away deep structural inequalities. You can make the case either way, depending which problem you choose, the story you want to tell about it, and the evidence you choose to highlight.

The final link in the chain of alignment is the policy intervention itself. Even where the problem definition is clear, and is seemingly in keeping with the evidence, and is supported by a strong narrative, it's still possible for governments to then select an intervention that doesn't meet the promise of the other three facets. Imagine a scenario in which a government decides that we must have more women on company boards as an equality measure. The data and evidence are strong that companies actually do better through this diversity. Ministers might put forward a narrative on how this is a measure that's good for both society and the economy. But then, as a policy intervention, their sole solution might be simply to 'encourage' more girls to do business subjects at school. It's a policy initiative doomed to failure because the proposed measure is out of alignment with the other three parts. The problem is clear, the data supports action, and the narrative is strong, but the policy intervention itself is a damp squib.

The equivalent for our youth drug-use scenario might be something similar. Let's say we adopted a problem definition suggesting that family breakdown was actually the greatest single cause of young people turning to drugs. We might be able to produce survey data showing a clear correlation between the two and refer to some academic studies isolating family breakdown as a causal driver. That would then underpin a narrative about groups of young people who feel lost without the emotional anchor that family provides. Having got those three ducks to align, a government might then apply a policy intervention that doesn't match. They might, for instance, decide to institute bag searches for drugs at school entrances. It's a solution that just doesn't line up with the other three parts.

The fascinating thing for governments is that getting all four ducks in a row not only underpins an increased chance of policy success, it also offers a much greater chance of *political* success. If politics is ultimately the art of persuasion – of convincing voters that your words and actions are making their lives better – then it is imperative that those words and actions align. That can actually be incredibly difficult. Sometimes the best our political leaders can manage is to achieve a partial success and then hold on tight. The ups and downs of President Obama's health-care policy in the USA reveals the hard politics that can swamp any row of policy ducks as they strive doggedly to get into line.

Every rose has its thorn. To some, this is simply a rather trite observation. For fans of the rock band Poison, it evokes deeper emotions. It was the title for the band's monster hit of 1988, reaching number one on the US billboard charts. In the era of power ballads and soulful looks, it struck a chord with mournful teenagers everywhere. For the band, and lead singer Bret Michaels, it was a moment of extraordinary triumph. What fewer people at the time knew was that Bret Michaels also quietly triumphed every day against his own particular health adversity. Bret Michaels has Type 1 diabetes. He has had to carefully monitor his blood-sugar levels ever since he was first diagnosed as a child, and injects insulin as and when required. Type 1 diabetes is not a disease that its sufferers can see coming. It does not result from a rock-'n'-roll lifestyle, but rather from fate's roll of the dice.

Judge Sonia Sotomayor of the US Supreme Court would no doubt understand. She too has Type 1 diabetes. Former British Prime Minister Theresa May, Pakistani cricket great Wasim Akram, and Nick Jonas of Jonas Brothers fame all understand the challenges of Type 1 diabetes from first-hand experience. They are amongst the millions of sufferers worldwide.

And it gets worse when we look at Type 2. There are many factors that contribute to Type 2 diabetes, which has often found itself labelled as a lifestyle disease, since being overweight increases the likelihood of developing it. The twenty-first century has seen Type 2 diabetes transform into something of a health juggernaut. According to the US Centers for Disease Control and Prevention, more than 30 million Americans now live with Type 2 diabetes.[2] India also has a combined total of more than 30 million people with either Type 1 or 2 diabetes.[3] According to the International Diabetes Federation, South Africa has more than four million adults with diabetes, representing more than 11 per cent of the adult population.[4] Across Europe, the total is now more than sixty million. Together, across the globe, an estimated half a billion people are living with diabetes.

Without proper treatment and care, the consequences can be grave. Diabetes can lead to eye disease and blindness, increased risks of heart disease, and even foot and lower leg amputations. The main treatment that diabetics rely on is the provision of insulin. Those of us lucky enough not to suffer with diabetes produce insulin naturally. Our bodies manufacture it for us and deploy it to keep blood sugar levels stable. Diabetics aren't so lucky. They have to constantly monitor their blood sugar through pin-prick tests, and if levels are dropping, they inject insulin to get things back in balance.

That level of discipline is tough on anyone. If you can't get easy access to insulin, it becomes dramatically tougher. In the UK, insulin – like other prescription medications – is available free on the National Health Service to those with appropriate certification. The same applies in Australia, where holders of a Healthcare card can access it at very low cost (with an extra safety net provision), and all Australians – regardless of income – can access heavily subsidized insulin through the pharmaceutical benefits scheme. Canada is similar, as are countries across Europe. All have what are called single-payer health insurance systems, which keep prices in check by regulating the market for pharmaceuticals.

Not so in the USA. With no national system, health insurance has become something of a minefield. Often, healthcare comes as part of the job package for employed Americans, but not always. This still leaves millions without health insurance coverage. And for everyone, drug prices seem to grow exponentially. That makes things challenging for people living with an illness like diabetes. As has been well publicized over the past few years, Americans with diabetes are having to make extraordinary decisions on how to keep supplying themselves with insulin.

In 2017, a young man in Minnesota named Alec Smith turned twenty-six. Accompanying the celebrations was the unfortunate reality that he ceased to be covered by his parents' health insurance. Within a month, Alec Smith was dead. A Type 1 diabetic, and unable to afford the cost of his insulin refill, he reportedly tried to ration his remaining supplies of the medicine to stretch it for longer. It proved a fatal decision. How could this tragedy have been allowed to happen? Wasn't the Obamacare law supposed to fix the problems of uninsured Americans and reduce those out-of-reach drug prices?

As always in public policy, the answer is more complex than

the narratives that were told about it. To understand why Obamacare didn't get its ducks in a row in a lasting way, we have to look all the way back to the presidential election campaign of 2008, when health insurance dominated as a major election issue. At the time, even the Democratic Party had not yet widely embraced those advocating for a broad-based, single-payer model of national health insurance. It was still seen as an idea that resided on the 'socialist fringe' of the party, nursed along by folks like Senator Bernie Sanders. Within a decade it would make its way into the mainstream. Nonetheless, already in 2008, what to do about the broken health-care system was front and centre in the national debate, and not just in the primaries. Republicans too were pulled into the discussion, and the eventual nominee John McCain went head-to-head with Obama on their competing plans on the issue.

Obama wanted universal coverage, but through a system of insurance exchanges, where everyone would be incentivized to select from a choice of public and private offerings. The overarching goal was to make sure that no one, rich or poor, would be denied a route to health insurance coverage, including those with pre-existing conditions. As early as January 2007, Obama was setting out his stall on the issue: 'In the 2008 campaign, affordable, universal health care for every single American must not be a question of whether, it must be a question of how.'[5] He suggested that the status quo was both 'morally offensive' and 'economically untenable'.

McCain was proposing something different. He wanted tax credits, and promised an easing of the restrictions preventing people from purchasing health insurance across state lines.

During the campaign, he framed it as being all about increasing choice for individuals and families: 'Senator Obama thinks we can improve health care by driving Americans into a new system of government orders, regulations and mandates. I believe we can make health care more available, affordable and responsive . . . by giving families more choices over their care.'[6]

So at the point of problem definition, there was already extensive disagreement on what the problem actually was. On the core issue – that millions of Americans did not have health insurance coverage – there was little disagreement. But identifying the underlying problem that was causing this undesirable outcome was a matter of fierce contestation. For Obama, the problem was that the open market was failing Americans seeking health care. There was simply no incentive for private companies to insure people who had expensive pre-existing health conditions. Someone with diabetes, for instance, was sure to attract a higher premium because of their ongoing, long-term need for insulin. What's more, for those Americans unable to access insurance as part of their job package, there was no easy road to getting health insurance at all. If they got sick, they had neither the savings nor the insurance to guarantee treatment. So the problem was essentially market failure. Too many Americans needed a service that no one would give them at a reasonable price. Greed was getting in the way. The only entity capable of stepping in to address that market failure was government itself.

For McCain, the problem wasn't this at all. The problem was not market failure but insufficient individual choice being given to Americans to choose the type and level of insurance that they needed. McCain suggested that Obama's 'plan represents the old ways of government. Mine trusts in the common sense of the American people.' It was a classic ideological split on the nature of social problems in general, applied in this case to health insurance. Should government get involved, or get out of the way?

Arguments over problem definition never really end, but the winners of democratic contests get the chance to turn their view of the problem into policy action. President Obama got that chance by virtue of his election victory, and he was determined to make the most of it. He started by making sure the narrative for action was strong. Obama was always a good storyteller. He consistently looked for the exemplars that would add a human face to political issues. He understood that politics is about emotion as well as facts. On the night that he won the presidency, he delivered a speech in Chicago's Grant Park in which he memorably invoked the story of Ann Nixon Cooper as a metaphor for America's capacity to change. As Obama told the crowd, Cooper had seen the best and worst of American history because she was 106 years old. She knew that America could change because she'd witnessed it over decades. Her personal story carried Obama's wider message about the type of country he was seeking to build.

He now looked for similar stories to carry the narrative for change on the US health-care system. He shared insights into the individual lives of doctors and patients, opening personal windows that could humanize complex policy arguments. He made the case for change by highlighting the poor results the current system was delivering: 'It's unsustainable for Americans like Laura Klitzka, a young mother that I met in Wisconsin just last week, who's learned that the breast cancer she thought she'd beaten had spread to her bones, but who's now being forced to spend time worrying about how to cover the $50,000 in medical debts she's already accumulated, worried about future debts that she's going to accumulate, when all she wants to do is spend time with her two children and focus on getting well. These are not the worries that a woman like Laura should have to face in a nation as wealthy as ours.'[7] In that same speech, delivered to the American Medical Association, Obama named a doctor who had to spend time on insurance paper-work that he could be spending on patients. He named small-business owners who'd had to lay off staff because they couldn't cover the health insurance for them. And, perhaps most powerfully of all, he recalled how his own mother had fought cancer whilst beset by fear that her insurer wouldn't cover her treatment.

These were powerful stories with which to shape a policy narrative. The data and evidence were also undeniable. Nobody from either major party was suggesting that the health-care system was delivering perfectly good results as it was. The status quo was a broken system. The Centers for Disease Control and Prevention released a report in 2008 stating that 43.8 million Americans were without health insur-ance.[8] There were also millions more who had some insurance but were not covered fully.

So for Obama, the first three ducks seemed well aligned in that first year of his presidency. His election had secured the temporary primacy of his problem definition. He had no trouble turning that problem into a narrative of how the lives of everyday Americans were being damaged – medically and financially – by an out-of-control system. And there was little dispute about the data and evidence. What proved to be the most troublesome of the ducks on this occasion was to shape an intervention that could somehow navigate the extraordinary politics of health care in the US.

The vested interests competing in American health care are vast. From large insurance companies, to powerful medical organizations, pharmaceutical companies, and the employer groups who have to pay for the cover of employees, there was a cacophony of voices seeking to give their preferred shape to any health-care deal. This was coupled with the political belief that any lasting health-care solution would need some bipartisan support. So even with control of both houses of Congress, Obama's first instinct was to seek some middle ground.

In September 2009, in his speech to Congress laying out his proposed law, Obama drew distinctions between the preferred plans of the left and the right as he saw them. The single-payer model on the left, and greater individual choice on the right, were the two options he canvassed. But he sought to paint them both as being too extreme: 'either one would represent a radical shift that would disrupt the health care most people currently have. Since health care represents one-sixth of our economy, I believe it makes more sense to build on what works and fix what doesn't, rather than try to build an entirely new system from scratch.'[9] This had not necessarily been Obama's preferred approach from the outset, but it was what he was left with after the political horse-trading of previous months. So there was a degree of misalignment locked in between Obama's original narrative about the problem, and the solution eventually arrived at. The story had been about universal coverage and the unacceptable cost of health care. The solution was unable to deliver it in full. The ducks refused to get in a row.

The core of the policy seemed easy enough to spell out. People who liked their existing health plans could keep them. Those who didn't, or who were uninsured, would be able to access a new insurance marketplace – the exchange – to get a private deal or take the public model. For those who couldn't afford this insurance, tax credits would be available. Perhaps most controversially, opting out was not in the brochure. To broaden the base, Obama's plan made it compulsory to hold insurance, so that all Americans would have some coverage.

The devil was in the detail. Once the policy started, surveys suggested that people weren't signing up because they weren't sure what the plan actually involved.[10] When the insurance exchange website went live, it crashed; it was consistently unable to handle the volume of traffic. Some insurance companies refused to participate. These are all what you might call implementation problems, but they also link back to the nature of the intervention itself. It was – of necessity – an extremely complex piece of policymaking with lots of moving parts. It was an imperfect grab-bag of measures. The Affordable Care Act had to navigate decades of American suspicion of big government. It also needed to thread the needle of a federal system, in which some states decided to go their own way and offer their own insurance option rather than impose the national one.

The politics have been intense ever since. As hyper-partisanship has taken hold in Washington, Republicans have refused to play ball on Obamacare. It started with the passage of the Affordable Care Act itself. After some initial positive engagement from Republicans at the negotiation stage, the final bill was passed entirely along party lines, with not a single Republican vote in the Senate. The great bipartisan achievement that Obama had visualized became instead a byword for partisan division. What's more, on the way through, he'd had to give up on the idea of the so-called 'public option' of a government-owned insurer, an idea he'd had to trade away in the search for Senate votes.

It hasn't got any easier. On several occasions, court cases have progressed all the way to the Supreme Court, amidst blazing publicity, failing to overturn the law in its entirety but nibbling remorselessly at its edges. Republicans in Congress have tried on many occasions to repeal the ACA, but have never quite been able to muster the numbers, particularly in key Senate votes. President Trump's rhetoric on the ACA was uncompromising throughout his term as he repeatedly expressed his determination to repeal and replace the legislation.

At the time of writing, a decade after the ACA became law, the results remain mixed. Tens of millions of Americans do not currently carry health insurance. The goal of universality has not been reached. Pharmaceutical costs are still up sharply, leading to extraordinary discrepancies between the price Americans pay and those paid in other advanced democracies. On the plus side, about 20 million more Americans than before now have insurance cover.[11] The evidence suggests that poorer Americans and those from minority backgrounds in particular have benefited. Perhaps most importantly, the law has ensured that people with pre-existing conditions are given a fighting chance. So some things are undoubtedly better. But just as self-evidently, some serious issues remain.

The improved levels of health insurance have also not resulted in the hoped-for lower medication prices, leading to the kind of insulin minefield that took the life of Alec Smith. His death revealed once more just how hard it is to get policy 'right' in a way that ensures nobody is missed. Alec Smith had a 'decent' job as a restaurant manager. He had a salary of $35,000 a year. This meant he was stuck in the gap of earning too much to qualify for government assistance, but too little to be able to afford an insurance package on the exchange to cover his needs. Without insurance, his insulin cost him over $1,000 a month, and he simply couldn't afford it. He paid for that reality with his life, and already his home state of Minnesota has passed the Alec Smith Insulin Affordability Act to try and make sure this situation can't happen again.

The fate of Obamacare shows how difficult it is to get the four ducks in a row in major reform initiatives. The problem definition remained fiercely contested. The data were clear enough that things were going wrong, and the policy narrative invoked simple stories of hardship that needed to be addressed. But the solution, when it came, got lost in its own complexity. It didn't align with the promise of the narrative, or match the full problem definition. The result has been a partial policy success – one that survives only because no coherent alternative has emerged that could realistically do better.

Public policy remains a very complex business. There are many reasons why citizens feel unhappy with their governments, and social scientists spend their lives producing the kind of rigorous studies needed to work out why. Citizens notice when governments haven't got it together. When there is misalignment between the facts and the message, or the problem and the solution, it dents trust. It means that different governments can implement much the same policies and yet find that some of them get punished by their citizens where others get praised. The difference is the clarity and consistency that comes from getting those ducks in a row.

This observation – and indeed this book – also comes with a warning attached. The four ducks are a means for improving the political chances of policy success. It is not a recipe or guarantee of *moral* or *ethical* policy in any wider sense. It is not a rational, objective, expert model designed to throw up measured solutions. It is simply a set of tools to uncover how governments approach the politics of policymaking.

This reflects something about the nature of knowledge. It is contextual. Problems are constructs created by humans to give shape to existing realities. What we say about those problems – the narrative shape that we give them – is a matter of choice. The evidence that we then examine to try and analyse those problems is never absolute. We all suffer from something that social scientist Herbert Simon called 'bounded rationality'. We can never really know everything about an issue, so we are left making imperfect decisions based on what we do know. What we know is also influenced by how we *feel* about it.

The impact of the alignment or misalignment of the four ducks has power whatever the type of policy problem being considered. This includes foreign policy decisions. Contrast, for example, public perception in the West about the US-led war in Afghanistan in 2001 and the US-led invasion of Iraq in 2003. The immense recent tragedy associated with the US withdrawal from Afghanistan in 2021 remains searingly fresh in our minds. Few people now view the US's two decades in Afghanistan as a foreign policy success story. This makes it easy to forget that twenty years ago, popular support for the beginning of that military intervention was high in the USA and allied countries.

Following the shattering events of 11 September 2001, when terrorists brought down the Twin Towers in New York, citizens sought the reassurance of a government response. It very quickly became clear that the terrorist group which later claimed responsibility – Osama Bin Laden's Al-Qaeda network – was being sheltered and supported by the Taliban regime in Afghanistan. The political narrative of the Bush administration suggested that the terrorists and the government protecting them needed to be chased out. The evidence linking the Taliban regime to support for terrorism was widely accepted across the globe. The policy intervention – in this case the use of military action – was supported by a very wide coalition of countries, all of which contributed personnel and resources in support of Operation Enduring Freedom and the subsequent setting up of the International Security Assistance Force. There was alignment between the 'problem', the evidence about what was going on, the political narratives being told about it, and the interventions proposed as a result.

Contrast that with the US-led invasion of Iraq less than two years later. The 'problem' as defined by the US and its closest allies was that Iraq under Saddam Hussein constituted a threat to world peace because of its weapons of mass destruction.

Their political narrative was built around that framing. The alignment issue was the lack of clear data and evidence in support of that narrative. The narrative was constantly under popular challenge because of the inability to provide clear evidence. The subsequent failure to find any weapons of mass destruction after the invasion only helped to cement the war in the public mind as – at best – a foreign policy failure and – at worst – an illegal use of force under international law.

The same factors apply in all sorts of domestic policy settings. Which brings me back to the case study which started this chapter: the exams debacle in the UK. It is easy in some ways to simply blame the decision-making of the individual ministers involved. Or similarly to lay the blame at the feet of the exams regulators for allowing things to proceed in the way that they did. Nevertheless, it is also notable that Scotland, Wales and England all backflipped on this only after they were forced into action by the public backlash. A Scottish National Party administration in Edinburgh, a Labour Party administration in Cardiff, and a Conservative Party administration in London all repeated the same mistake. So, if it was an error of individual competence, there seems to have been an extraordinary spate of it. In other circumstances, such bipartisan consistency might be considered refreshing.

Whether or not using teacher-assessed grades was ultimately the *right* or the *best* policy outcome in some objective sense remains debatable. The governments were proven right in their predictions that grade inflation would happen without an algorithm to combat it. So their data and evidence was 'correct' as far as it goes. But it didn't align with either the narrative or the actual interventions adopted. The narrative was all about a fair and appropriate assessment regime. That did not align with the lived reality on the ground, with the problem as people actually experienced it. The governments were solving the wrong problem. They saw the problem as avoiding unrepresentative grades. The real issue was how to create a system that would be accepted as 'fair' when the normal exams were not able to provide it. It was only when a policy solution to *that* problem was adopted that the four ducks realigned themselves. By then, the political damage had already been done.

1. Problems, Problems, Problems

New York City is a busy place. The cars, the people, the noise. It's called the city that never sleeps for a reason. Allen Street is no exception. On the lower east side of Manhattan, close to Chinatown, the flow of people is constant. Packed traffic contends with parked cars and general madness. Allen Street is not the kind of place that leaps to mind as a venue for secret activities. Not unless you prefer your secrets to be hiding in plain sight.

In early October 2013, Allen Street quietly made its way into the international headlines. The action centred on number 18, although not because the paparazzi had captured some insanely famous celebrity in residence there. Quite the opposite. It was what a celebrity had left behind that was causing the interest. What turned up at 18 Allen Street was a quite stunning piece of graffiti, showing two street urchins reaching up towards a 'no graffiti' sign. What emerged almost immediately was the extra news that this picture was the work of Banksy, perhaps the most famous graffiti artist in the world.

Banksy was engaged in a self-described 'residency on the streets of New York' in October 2013. At least two things made this unique compared to your average artist-in-residence arrangement. The first was that Banksy's art was invariably produced on buildings that belonged to other people, and not at their invitation. The second was that Banksy's identity remained unknown, the adventurous Zorro of the art world who never let the mask slip. The picture at 18 Allen Street was the first of many to emerge in the weeks that followed.

Not everyone was pleased. Within days, the piece in Allen Street had been painted over. Some elected officials were wary of the whole business. New York City Mayor Mike Bloomberg certainly wasn't a fan. 'You running up to somebody's property or public property and defacing it is not my definition of art.'[1] He insisted that it was in fact against the law. The public, of course, voted with their feet, and rushed to view each new work as it was discovered. Other graffiti artists vied to tag the works, and critics trying to paint them over got into physical altercations with their would-be defenders.

Is there a public policy problem here? It depends on who you ask. Where you sit depends on where you stand. For some, street art is exactly that – art. For others, it is gratuitous vandalism. Mike Bloomberg said it was bad for property values. He may be right. But so too is living next door to people who don't take care of their front yards. Should we make that illegal too?

Is the problem not so much the artwork, but where it occurs? Rome, the eternal city, has for the last two decades been considered something of a graffiti magnet. Buildings that have fascinated the world for millennia now find themselves surrounded by spray-paint from the rebels of the twenty-first century. If we simply leave the graffiti, will people in five hundred years' time think of the works themselves as part of the layered history of Rome? Art does not stand still. Like all reputations, those of artists wax and wane according to the fashion of the day. But that is part of the matrix of decision-making too. Would Mayor Bloomberg have been asked about the graffiti at all if it had been painted by street artists who have not yet made a name for themselves?

Graffiti is just one of the many thousands of subjects about which politicians argue in most places on earth. In reality, these arguments are acts of problem definition, an attempt to frame an issue on the preferred terms of the person doing the talking. Is graffiti great art, and its appearance on public buildings an expression of egalitarian values? Could be. Should it rather be seen as vandalism that is destroying people's house values and undermining law-abiding cultures of civility? Perhaps. The answer is never straightforward because the answer is political. It is rooted in the ideological worldview of the beholder and is inevitably shaped by the political context of the day. The way that discussion goes will have deep reper-cussions for what happens next. It's only a problem if the politics of the day is willing to identify it as a problem. That discussion is the entry point, the moment that determines whether the first duck starts to swim.

Problem definition is all about the rhetoric that politicians and interest groups use to frame a particular issue for public consumption. Policy problems are in the eye of the beholder. They are influenced by politics as much as they are by data and evidence. Take something like unemployment. For believers in individual responsibility, freedom of choice and the free market, the 'problem' of unemployment is best solved by actually 'encouraging' people to work by limiting their welfare benefits. There's no virtue, this argument goes, in creating cultures of dependency where people just look to government for a handout if they lose their jobs. The same mindset underpinned the Victorian poor law, which sought to make workhouses such unappealing places that only the utterly destitute would consider turning to them for help. For today's inheritors of that thinking, the 'problem' of unemployment is essentially one of laziness and an unwillingness by the unemployed to take the jobs that are on offer.

The competing problem definition is entirely different. It suggests that there are not actually enough jobs available, coupled with insufficient investment in the skills that allow people to compete for the jobs that do exist. The alternative definition also stresses that social inequality underpins joblessness. People fighting to simply stay alive on the wrong side of the poverty line don't have the same job opportunities as a recent graduate of Cambridge or Harvard.

Both sides of the argument purport to define the same basic problem that we know as 'unemployment', framed from two totally different perspectives. All policy problems are framed this way, and the definitions adopted inevitably lead to particular types of policy intervention. That's why politicians and interest groups invest so much in their public messaging – they are literally fighting to embed a particular version of a problem in the public mind. That's how the definition game works.

It doesn't seem that long ago that Justin Trudeau took the world by storm. For a brief moment, the Canadian prime minister didn't just embody the zeitgeist, he seemed to own it. Young, photogenic, dynamic, charismatic and optimistic, he was also something of a political clean slate. Despite being the son of one of Canada's most iconic former prime ministers, the younger Trudeau had only slowly and seemingly reluctantly found his way into politics. But then his rise was rapid. Elected leader of the Liberal Party in 2013, he led it to a surging majority victory in 2015 in an enormous electoral turnaround.

Amongst his campaign promises, there was a commitment to fundamental reform of the Canadian electoral system. In Canada, as in the UK and many other places, national elections are run on what is known as the 'first-past-the-post' system. Essentially it means that whoever gets the most votes in a contest is the winner, regardless of whether the majority of eligible voters actually chose them. All that is required is a plurality of votes. If candidate X gets 23 per cent of the vote, candidate Y gets 22 per cent, and candidate Z gets 21 per cent, it is candidate X who gets the win – despite the fact that the other two combined got 43 per cent of the vote and candidate X got less than a quarter of the whole. It is representative democracy in its most basic and unsophisticated form. It means that governments can win a majority of seats in Parliament without having to win a majority of votes. Even when elected in a landslide in 2015, Trudeau's Liberals won majority government with only 39 per cent of the vote.

Does it matter?

The reason the system survives is largely a political one. It is seen – rightly – as a system that favours major parties. Significant minority parties might win a strong percentage of the national vote, but no seats at all, because they can't concentrate enough votes in a single seat to get past the majority party candidate. And herein lays the dilemma: there is no incentive for major parties to try and reform a system which is biased in their favour.

The second issue is that the system is seen as delivering stronger majoritarian governments. Supporters say that this gives ministers a better chance to deliver on their promises and govern well, without having to negotiate everything through the complexity of smaller parties that exist in countries with proportional voting systems. Critics point out that in reality this system delivers lots of minority governments too, as the second and third terms of the Trudeau government demonstrate.

Trudeau came to power pledging that things would change. He promised, in fact, that the 2015 election itself would be the last one to be held under the existing first-past-the-post system. The promise was included as a centrepiece of the Liberal campaign, and then reiterated in the governor-general's speech from the throne for the new government: 'To make sure that every vote counts, the Government will undertake consultations on electoral reform, and will take action to ensure that 2015 will be the last federal election conducted under the first-past-the-post voting system.'[2]

It all started well. A cross-party committee was formed in mid-2016 to look at alternative voting regimes. The committee toured Canada to take verbal submissions, producing a final report and recommendations that were delivered to Parliament at the start of December 2016. They recommended moving to some form of proportional representation, with the new system to be endorsed by referendum. It seemed to be a by-the-book recipe for policy success. And then, suddenly, it wasn't.

Trudeau walked away. What went wrong? The challenge with any policy change, even one of this magnitude, is to be able to clearly define the problem and then build a narrative towards its solution. The problem here was that there was no problem; at least not a clearly defined one. The staunchest criticisms of the first-past-the-post system invariably come from the smaller parties who would benefit from proportional representation and win more seats. For them it's both a political problem and a democratic one. But it has proven difficult to state that problem in a way that gets the majority of voters really excited about the issue.

Electoral reform sounds important to public policy scholars like me, but can easily seem a bit niche to everyone else. We know that's true in Canada because every time they've been asked about it, the public have tended to vote no. One of Canada's largest provinces, British Columbia, held a referendum on whether the local legislature should get rid of first-past-the-post, and the people said no. In fact, they said no three times. In a 2001 referendum, they managed 57 per cent support for change, but fell short of the 60 per cent threshold they needed at the time. At a second referendum in 2009, they could only muster 40 per cent support for change. A third referendum in 2018 saw a near repeat of that result, with 61 per cent of voters against change. Prince Edward Island also had a referendum in 2019, and support for change there stalled at 48 per cent. The hard truth is that not enough Canadian voters see the electoral system as a problem. And without a problem to fix, Justin Trudeau decided not to spend his political capital on an 'unnecessary' policy intervention.

Had the proposal for a national referendum gone ahead,

what would its chances of success have been? The Angus Reid Institute conducted polling on the issue in both 2016 and 2019.[3] Overall in 2016, the figures suggested that there was 47 per cent support for change, but with only 28 per cent of Conservative Party voters in favour. By 2019, having just lost a close election in which their party actually won more votes than the Liberals, Conservative voters seemed to have changed their minds, with 69 per cent in favour of reform. The Liberal voters were 49 per cent in favour in 2016 and 55 per cent in favour in 2019. By far the biggest support – unsurprisingly – came from minority party voters who thought a new system would better reflect the support that exists for their parties. This included 83 per cent of Green Party voters and 86 per cent of New Democratic Party voters in 2019.

The politics of the issue are tricky. As has been shown by referendums held in Canadian provinces, the final votes are much closer than early polling in favour of reform would predict. Once lobbying on the question gets intense, and reform proposals move from theoretical questions to looming practical realities, voters get spooked. That's not unusual. The UK had a similar experience when holding a national referendum in 2011 on whether to move away from the first-past-the-post system to what is known as an 'alternative vote' (AV) system. In essence the 'alternative vote' just means voters get to list the candidates in order of their preference, rather than having to plump for their first choice only. It's the system used for Australian national elections for the lower house. Early polls in the UK in 2010 suggested that there was greater support for change than for the status quo. But after a bitterly fought referendum campaign, voters chose to stick with the devil they knew. When push came to shove, the 'no' vote in the referendum itself was a whopping 67.9 per cent.

So Canada's struggles with electoral reform are far from unique. In New Zealand, which now has proportional representation, they had a series of referendums in the early 1990s to narrow down the options. In a first referendum in 1992, 84.7 per cent of voters said they wanted a different system to first-past-the-post. Come decision day in the final referendum in 1993, only 53.9 per cent actually voted for change. It just shows that defining a problem in the electoral system sufficiently clearly to force through a policy change is really difficult, even when there is strong initial buy-in. Canadians might take some comfort from the fact that people tend to relax a little once the jump has actually been made. In New Zealand, a follow-up referendum in 2012 confirmed 58 per cent support for keeping the proportional system.

And in Canada the debate is certainly not over. Even in 2016/17, as the Liberals walked away from change, the supporters of proportional representation were determined to go down swinging. The organization Fair Vote Canada has been campaigning for the change to proportional representation since 2001, and they threw themselves into the consultation process following Trudeau's initial electoral victory. They mustered an extensive and impressive array of data and evidence in support of their case. There was no shortage of disappointment from supporters of change who felt that Trudeau had failed a leadership test by abandoning the issue. Writing in the *Policy Options* magazine in 2017, Kelly Carmichael from Fair Vote Canada rounded on the prime minister for showing 'Canadians that he did not possess the leadership qualities required to champion a fairer system. He chose the allure of another false majority, and the fortunes of his party over Canadian democracy.'[4]

At the time of writing, no provincial or federal government in Canada has been successful in winning a referendum to dismantle first-past-the-post voting. Despite all the arguments and the broken promises, currently the verdict of the majority of Canadians is 'no problem'. The coalition of voices against change has won the battle of problem definition against the alternative view. That's not because those in favour of change are 'wrong' in their arguments – because it's not about right or wrong. Success relies on being able to persuasively frame a policy problem in ways that drive political action. That's how politics works. Without that successful ability to define the problem, the first duck never leaves safe harbour.

'Why did they throw the food at me? I am not an animal. I am a human.' These are the words of a Mexican immigrant to the USA who participated in a University of Denver study on the experiences of Latinos in Colorado.[5] The person in question, known only as participant E, had been ordering food at a restaurant. The study is one of many that have shown just how hard it is for first-generation Mexican immigrants in the USA to find acceptance and the better life that they crave. Undocumented immigrants in particular, fighting joblessness, and living in fear of discovery by the authorities, have found no easy harbour in the United States.

The last decade has seen fierce debate over the vilification of the figure of 'the immigrant' in many parts of the world. In debates on both sides of the Atlantic, some political parties and sizeable segments of the voting public have begun to see immigrants from poorer countries as a threat. The perceived threat is economic, social and cultural, and has fed into the rise of a resurgent nationalism in the Brexit debates in the UK, in many countries of the EU, and under the Trump presidency in the USA.

The 'othering' of immigrants is certainly not a new phenomenon, and the contemporary debate is simply the latest manifestation of the struggles for acceptance that immigrants have long faced in almost all countries. A dispassionate look at the evidence suggests that immigration is in fact a tremendous driver of economic growth and cultural enrichment. But problem definition is a political activity, and politics is at core an emotional business. This is always apparent in discussions around immigration, and never more so than during election campaigns.

The 2016 presidential campaign in the US – like its 2020 successor – was an extraordinary event. What made it extraordinary was the Republican candidate. Everything about Donald Trump made his campaign unusual. No one had ever won the US presidency by insulting war heroes like John McCain, and belittling many others in his own party, whilst facing down revelations about shockingly inappropriate language on the treatment of women. But what Trump also had was a compelling and powerful wider narrative about an American dream allegedly being torn apart. It was a story of stolen opportunities, broken industries, and borders that were not being respected. The policy promise that most gave shape to that story was his determination to build a wall along the entire border with Mexico.

The wall isn't really a 'thing' at all – notwithstanding that some sections were eventually built. The main purpose of the wall is as a symbol, a metaphor, a vehicle designed to carry all the problems of modern America and drive them to the Mexican border. Throughout his campaign, and then underpinned by his extraordinary inaugural speech, Trump had set up a meta narrative of American decline. The anxieties of those Americans who felt they were being ignored, or their lives were going backwards, were prodded by Trump's rhetoric. Like a sore that you can't stop picking, Trump kept poking at this sense of decline and malaise.

But he needed specific policy areas in which to crystallize this general story. Places where he could reassert American control in the eyes of his supporters. He found that place at the border.

The US border with Mexico is like the graffiti issue at the start of this chapter. What you see depends on where you look. Trump was able to create a problem definition that got enough Americans to look at the border as a 'problem' in the same way he did. George Lakoff, in his wonderful little book *Don't Think of an Elephant*, writes about the power of words which come preloaded with embedded meanings – known as 'frames' – that the listener then reacts to. Trump's wall is exactly one of these preloaded frames. What is a wall for? It's for keeping things out and for keeping those on the inside safe. The great big wall was Trump's way to trigger the emotions of anxious Americans into thinking that he would keep them safe. His wall would solve America's problems by stopping unwanted arrivals.

All problems come in pieces, and politicians try to put them together for us in ways that will make us buy into their world-view. So in seeking to define the problem of the Mexican border, Trump started by looking at a different problem altogether: crime. Most of us are worried about crime in some way. Nobody likes to feel unsafe. Trump's first building block was the idea that having a great big wall at the border would contribute to stopping crime. How? Well, by stopping criminals from entering the United States. 'When Mexico sends its people, they're not sending their best . . . They're bringing drugs. They're bringing crime. They're rapists.' This was Trump's opening salvo in June 2015 on the day he announced he was running for president.

Problem definition is not necessarily about the 'truth' but simply about a perception of a segment of the truth – a segment that is capable of being framed into a problem.

The Washington Post published an article in July 2015, attempting to fact-check Trump's claims about Mexicans and crime. They found that a problem definition of this kind is incredibly difficult to 'fact-check' because it isn't really about the facts. This first duck is just about getting people to believe there is a problem that needs addressing. The *Post* concluded that: 'Trump's repeated statements about immigrants and crime underscore a common public perception that crime is correlated with immigration, especially illegal immigration. But that is a misperception; no solid data support it, and the data that do exist negate it.'[6] That analysis is undoubtedly 'correct', but that didn't negate Trump's ability to frame up a policy problem in his preferred terms. The *perception* was all he needed in order to define the problem and get the first duck moving.

In addition to crime, another issue on which Trump tapped into the anxieties of America was unemployment and low-paid jobs. The industrial decline of the American Midwest is well documented. Jobs that were once jobs for life have become precarious or have disappeared altogether. Once-thriving cities have given way to the 'rust belt' (a region of the United States that has seen industrial decline and falling populations since the 1980s), which has left people deeply concerned about their ability to make a living. Trump didn't invent that feeling. He simply harnessed it by suggesting that one of the things costing those American jobs was the number of undocumented immigrants 'flooding' into the country.

So, in building his definition of the policy problem of undocumented immigrants from Mexico allegedly pouring into the United States, Trump bundled together a bunch of anxieties, and rolled them up into one 'problem' demanding policy action. His proposed intervention was then breathtakingly simple. It swept away all the complexity of the issue by advocating the building of a great big wall. That intervention aligned well with his problem definition, and with the wider narrative he was propounding about it. Three out of the four ducks were swimming. What was out of whack was the data and evidence on the extent of the problem and the actual utility of a wall as a solution, which is why the fourth duck stayed in port and denied him full political victory on the issue.

Australia has an international reputation for enviable lifestyles and never-ending sunshine. Its people are friendly, its wildlife uniquely endearing, and its vast open spaces the stuff of legend.

Its houses, too, are known for being big. The large home on a quarter-acre-block, just waiting for the backyard barbecues to get under way, is inscribed into the Australian psyche. It might be an unrealistic caricature, but for much of the twentieth century it was a caricature underpinned by more than a whiff of reality. It formed the core of what has been known colloquially as the 'great Australian dream'. In the twenty-first century, that housing picture is now very much changing.

Take Sydney, for example. For many decades, the inner-city streets of Sydney used to be pretty rough neighbourhoods. For much of the 1900s, people who admitted to growing up in suburbs like Surry Hills and Redfern were not trying to brag about their social status. Such suburbs were working-class melting pots of new migrants and Indigenous Australians, often struggling in the face of disadvantage, poverty, and social dislocation. People who came into money were likely to spend it trying to get out of Redfern and Surry Hills.

These suburbs still retain many of their original terrace houses, thrown up in the late nineteenth and early twentieth centuries. Mean houses on small blocks, these were homes for people who were not in a position to demand anything better. Waterloo Street in Surry Hills is a good example. Interspersed amongst more modern office blocks are rows of terrace houses, all built right on the street, with little or no front yard. Look at the grainy old black-and-white photos of life in 1920s and 1930s Australia, and such terraces loom in the background, as large families congregate in the front and children play in the street.

Things have changed somewhat. In 2017 a terrace house in Waterloo Street sold for $1.6 million Australian dollars.

And not just any house. In order to even get it on the market, some new beams had to be installed to hold up the staircase and ceilings. Some floors were collapsed, and the state of the house was such that the estate agent felt physically ill when valuing it. Potential buyers had to sign a waiver to be allowed in. None of this was enough to put off buyers in modern-day Australia. The house sold in less than a week.[7]

In the twenty-first century, places like Surry Hills and Redfern have succumbed to the process of gentrification. Their proximity to the city has made them extraordinarily highly sought after. A similar process has been visible in most great cities around the world. Prices rise exponentially, driving out 'average' buyers, who simply can no longer compete in such a market. It is the dream of almost all young people to one day own a house of their own. It's almost a primal instinct. But it's getting harder because house prices have grown exponentially almost everywhere across the past two decades.

The problem in Australia is that increasingly the buyers being priced out of central locations have almost nowhere else to go either. House price inflation has not restricted itself just to the inner-city pads of well-to-do trendsetters, but has engulfed even the vast newer suburbs of all of Australia's major cities. At the time of writing, the median house price in Sydney is well over AUD$1 million, whilst median personal income is closer to $50,000. The financial maths would seem to defy economic logic, and yet price growth surges on. The global financial crisis and more recently the Covid pandemic have barely caused a blip in the seemingly interminable rise of Australian house prices. In February 2021, in the middle of the pandemic, Australian house prices surged by 2 per cent in a single month, the fastest growth in nearly two decades.[8] The million-dollar question for policymakers – quite literally – is whether all of this constitutes a policy problem.

It is rare that any issue is a problem for everyone. Public policy is about making choices, and that begins in the very act of problem definition itself. At one level, house price growth is good because homeowners become wealthier, at least on paper. Those who own their own home have enjoyed watching their wealth grow and are wary of seeing that stripped away. In the UK, a former architect of Tony Blair's New Labour project, Peter Mandelson, rather famously once declared that 'we are intensely relaxed about people getting filthy rich as long as they pay their taxes.' Successive Australian governments have taken a rather similar view to the extraordinary rises in house prices over the last two decades. The resultant stamp-duty taxes have brought wealth pouring into state government coffers.

Both major political parties in Australia agree that there is a housing affordability problem. But they have often framed that problem as being about incomes and access to deposits rather than house prices themselves being too high. That problem definition has proven remarkably resilient and has led to interventions like grants for first-home buyers, rather than interventions to actually bring prices down. When interventions that might actually lower prices have been suggested, they've struggled to gain traction with the electorate. The relative policy stability reflects the fact that the ducks remain in alignment, and no sufficiently persuasive alternative problem definition has emerged to change that.

The then Treasurer (and later Prime Minister) Scott

Morrison addressed the issue in 2017, considering ways to boost the money available to first-home buyers: 'The problem is being able to save quickly enough to get a deposit which is big enough to actually get yourself into the market . . . In Australia our prices may be high, particularly in Sydney and Melbourne, but they're real. The issue on housing affordability and prices in Australia is the mismatch between supply and demand. It's not the function of any sort of investor credit bubble or anything like this.'[9]

The Liberal Party, the major centre-right party in Australian politics, went on to use house prices as the basis of a political campaign against the opposition Labor Party in the 2019 election campaign, saying that house prices would fall under Labor. The proposed policy change at the heart of the debate was a Labor plan to abolish tax breaks – called 'negative gearing' – for investors buying properties in order to rent them out. Negative gearing had been supported by successive governments in Australia for decades, and many small-time 'mum and dad' investors had used it to build small portfolios of investment properties. Negative gearing had become established as a bit of a symbol of how 'ordinary' Australians could build wealth.

Labor had attempted for two elections in a row (2016 and 2019) to frame the housing problem as being about too many incentives for investors, artificially inflating prices to levels that were driving would-be first-home buyers out of the market. That attempted problem definition naturally led to proposed policy interventions to decrease investor incentives by limiting the available tax breaks. When first suggesting the changes in 2016, then Labor leader Bill Shorten spoke of putting 'the great Australian dream back within reach of working and middle-class Australians, who have been priced out of the market for too long.' Labor's Treasury spokesman, Chris Bowen, underlined that 'the tax system should not support someone buying their fifth, sixth or seventh house more than someone buying their first.'[10]

The challenge for Labor was that not enough homeowners saw house price growth as a problem. Many simply saw it as their own wealth increasing. In a country which still has relatively high home-ownership levels by world standards, not enough voters were willing to take the risk of seeing the value of their own home fall. In political terms, it didn't matter whether house prices would actually have fallen or not, because Labor lost the battle of problem definition. The policy was quietly dropped in 2021.

Of course, political parties aren't the only organizations involved in the definition of public policy problems. There is a coterie of think tanks, non-governmental organizations (NGOs), lobby groups and consultants who join in the game. Each enters the lists with a specific agenda and to push a particular point of view. So too in the battle to define the nature of Australia's housing affordability 'problem' and its relationship to high house prices. For example, the policy think tank the Grattan Institute in Melbourne warned in 2021 that the housing market was dividing people into 'haves and have-nots', with people increasingly relying on wealth from their parents to be able to cobble together a home deposit of their own.[11] But for those who are amongst the 'haves', things look good. Who doesn't want to see the value of what they own go up? For policymakers, higher house prices help to drive economic growth and tax revenue, which is a heady combination for any government looking to be re-elected.

It's a dilemma that has so far proven too hard to unpick. As the Head of the Economic Analysis Department at the Reserve Bank of Australia put it in a speech in 2008: 'At one level, rising housing prices have made many people feel wealthier and have contributed to higher levels of consumer spending than might otherwise have occurred.'[12] It's only a problem if the politics of the day allows it to be a problem. As economist Cameron Murray put it in a 2021 media interview: 'The political reality is that we want higher and rising house prices, it's a political winner and doing something to stop that is political suicide.'[13]

As is so often the case, housing affordability is really a set of multiple problems running in tandem. These problems are so intertwined that they trap policymakers into trying to address them as one coherent whole. The first issue is a problem of intergenerational inequality. The second and related problem is one of housing affordability. The third is a problem of people buying houses that they can't afford, leading to financial precarity. There are undoubtedly more. What these problems lack is a clear definition that allows for easy policy change. For the time being, the dominant problem definition remains the idea that first-home buyers lack the funds to break into the market. That's a problem that governments can fix by finding ways to get more money into the pockets of would-be buyers. First-home-buyer grants, loan guarantees for those with small deposits, and plans to allow people to draw down their superannuation are all aimed at getting people into the market without driving down prices.

The result, of course, is that house values keep growing, because the market simply prices in the extra money that first-home buyers get access to. It's either a virtuous cycle or a vicious spiral, depending on your point of view. And it all stems from the way the problem has been framed at the outset.

Not all problems present themselves to the public gaze so slowly and dispassionately. The debate about house prices in Australia has been bubbling along for at least two decades. It has never yet quite crystallized into a problem of such clear definition that action to stop house prices growing becomes inevitable. The same could be said for the Canadian electoral system. Different parties have tried to get the topic onto the public agenda for decades. Debates erupt, sometimes referendums occur, but the only constant so far has been the lack of action. The problem has not yet been defined compellingly enough to create a burning need for change.

Many problems swim along beneath the surface of our collective attention. We sort of know they are there, but we look the other way. What can change things is often a single event that cuts through the surface of our attention. What if, for example, a Canadian election was held in which a party somehow managed to gain a parliamentary majority with only 15 per cent of the vote? Suddenly what has seemed like a bearable problem might become something else.

In other words, problems that seemed under control or were simply out of sight can leap onto the policy agenda at a moment's notice. Tragedy and crisis can put them there. A horrific single crime can galvanize communities into suddenly demanding wider action. These are focusing events for public attention.

*

Rana Plaza is a place name seared into international memory. At least it should be. In 2013, this eight-storey building in the Savar area outside Dhaka in Bangladesh collapsed into rubble. As it descended in on itself, the structure took with it literally thousands of people. Over 1,100 people died and a further 2,500 people were injured in the collapse of this one building.[14] Most of the victims were garment workers, some of the millions of Bangladeshis who work to produce clothes for the world's best-known fashion houses at rates of pay that would shock most people in the world's advanced economies.

The main reason the building collapsed was because of structural failure. There had been warning signs, including the appearance the day before of enormous cracks in one side of the building. A fateful decision was made that people should come back to work the next day regardless. Tragedy ensued. Like so many tragedies, it was one that could so easily have been avoided.

It was a focusing event. Sweat-shop conditions had existed in the clothing industry for many years before this particular building collapsed. Building regulations had been deficient and inspection regimes poor. Western fashion houses did not take sufficient interest in the conditions under which their clothes were being manufactured. None of these things were unknown before the day that the Rana Plaza came down. But the tragedy of that moment forced the world to stop and take notice.

Problems do not emerge from nothing. They are 'discovered', but the discovery often results from a single galvanizing event like this that draws attention to an issue that has long been there. The events are dramatic, often tragic, and can act as important drivers for change. But such events are not acts of problem definition in themselves. They expose very real problems, but not yet in a form easily capable of resolution through policy action. The action comes as competing forces set out to explain what the actual problems are that have 'allowed' this event to occur.

The Rana Plaza tragedy forced policymakers in Bangladesh to identify the policy problems that had allowed the disaster to happen. This included poor building practices, lax regulation, insufficient oversight and inspection regimes, and overcrowded working conditions. International clothing brands were also forced to take some responsibility as their reputations suffered an impact.

Such events are not simply a Bangladeshi problem. Nor are such problems restricted simply to developing countries. In June 2017, a block of flats in London caught fire. A blaze in a single kitchen spread with alarming speed throughout the whole of Grenfell Tower, a building of twenty-four storeys. The inferno mercilessly claimed the lives of seventy-two people, injured at least seventy more and sent more than 200 scrambling for safety. The reason the fire spread so far and so fast was because the cladding on the outside of the building proved to be highly flammable. Fire safety concerns had been voiced in the years prior, but to no avail. The lack of action cost lives.[15]

The searingly tragic killings of individuals can have a similar impact in ensuring that policymakers cannot simply divert their gaze from the problems that are revealed. Terrible events like the murder of George Floyd in Minneapolis in 2020, the rape and murder of Sarah Everard as she walked home in

London in 2021, Rachel Thulborn being stabbed to death in front of her children in the Australian state of Queensland in 2008: the violent taking of life in each case drew public attention. It forced people to ask themselves – 'how could we allow this to happen?', and to demand action from governments in response. Not because the problems themselves were new or unknown, but because at that moment society could no longer bear them.

The truth is that black Americans have confronted embedded racism for centuries. Women have felt unsafe in the streets of towns and cities for centuries. Domestic partners have been fearing for their lives in violent relationships for centuries. It was suffering that was hiding in plain sight. But the galvanizing event in each case forced the issue into the public gaze. The enduring problem, tragically, is that immediate promises of government action have a depressing tendency to dissipate once the media attention moves on. At the time of writing, four years after the Grenfell fire, there are still UK apartment blocks covered in flammable cladding. More black Americans have died at the hands of law enforcement since George Floyd's murder. Many more women have been killed in both public and domestic settings since the shocking deaths of Sarah Everard and Rachel Thulborn. These human faces of suffering have the power to jolt us, but that jolt does not in itself guarantee action. Whether these tragic events drive actual policy change will depend on whether governments can be successfully pushed to offer viable solutions.

Once a problem emerges onto the public agenda, the battles of problem definition begin, but that is only the start. The other ducks are needed to line up and actually force the policy needle to move. That begins with constructing a narrative about why action needs to happen and what change might look like. These policy stories drive things forward through the kind of tales that make complex problems seem clearer and more actionable.

2. Tell Me a Story

The night was 27 June 2019, and the mercury was nudging close to 30 degrees in the city of Miami, Florida. On the debate stage that evening were no fewer than ten hopefuls vying for the right to be the Democratic nominee for president of the United States. Ten sounds like a lot. But in truth there were twenty-five candidates running. Of these, twenty qualified for the first debate, which had to be split over two nights to give everyone some kind of chance to speak. On the stage were senators, a former governor, a member of Congress, and the mayor of South Bend Indiana. Standing out in this crowd required more than just making a good policy argument. Data and evidence weren't going to do it by themselves either. Somebody had to tell a story.

The breakout speaker that evening was the then senator from California, Kamala Harris. Joe Biden had consistently sought in his campaign to play up his credentials as someone who had the capacity to reach across the aisle and work with his political enemies when necessary. He talked about having worked with segregationist former Democratic senators to get things done, despite his own very different views. As the discussion turned to the subject of race, Kamala Harris made a telling intervention. Speaking directly to Biden, she took him to task for working alongside people who had done so much to make the lives of African Americans harder. She could have made her point in so many different ways. She could have cited data on the number of black students who had suffered at the hands of segregationist policies. She could have set out a policy critique of the emotional, social and economic damage that discriminatory policies of the past had caused. She chose instead to do something even more powerful. She told a story.

'There was a little girl in California who was part of the second class to integrate her public schools, and she was bussed to school every day. And that little girl was me.'

In the space of just two short sentences, Harris was able to provide an insight into the pain, injustice and fear faced by generations of African American children who had confronted embedded racial discrimination in their schooling. But, just as importantly, that narrative was interlaced with a story of hope – of overcoming adversity. The 'little girl', who had been confronted by such emotionally testing moments just in order to go to school, was today standing on a debate stage running for office as the president of the United States. Now that is a powerful narrative.

For thousands of years, there has been one constant about the way that people communicate: humans are storytellers. It's the basis for how we understand our world. Storytelling – the creation of a 'narrative' around a problem – also helps politicians to cement a particular view of issues in the public mind. These stories help to underpin the problem definition, preparing the public mind for the policy solutions that are to follow.

Policy might not immediately seem like the stuff of story-books. At first glance, there are not too many knights in shining armour here. But on closer inspection, that is exactly what we find. As the social scientist Deborah Stone has explained, narrative stories in policymaking 'have heroes and villains and innocent victims, and they pit the forces of evil against the forces of good'.[1] Once we start looking, we find stories everywhere. Take Donald Trump's inaugural address. He referred to 'rusted-out factories scattered like tombstones across the landscape of our nation', and 'young and beautiful students deprived of knowledge'. He was determined to be the hero that would stop this 'American carnage'.

Putting to one side the sweeping nature of inaugural addresses, politicians are always telling stories. They hunger for metaphors and similes like the desert thirsts for water . . . and often with about as much subtlety. Successful stories are ultimately judged by their capacity to be persuasive. They must capture the moment and give shape to a policy problem in a way that has listeners nodding to themselves, muttering under their breath that 'this makes sense'. Stories are what link the description of a problem and the proposed solution, often through the use of an emotional hook.

We've all experienced the magic of a good story. It's one in which we get into the mindset of the lead characters and find ourselves cheering for them as they face seemingly insurmountable obstacles. When Harry Potter faces Voldemort, we are in no doubt about where our allegiances should be. We've been taken there by the story. Politicians are trying to do the same thing. They are painting stories of injustice designed to get us cheering for their solution, complete with emotional buy-in. A good story can move political mountains. The wrong story can lead to a political car crash. No story, and things are unlikely to move at all.

Back in 2002, the chair of the Conservative Party in the UK was a particularly talented person named Theresa May. Destined to go on and be a future prime minister, in 2002 her party was in opposition and her job was to tell a few home truths. Having been destroyed at the ballot box two elections in a row by Tony Blair's seemingly unstoppable 'New Labour' party, the Conservatives were experiencing a reflective moment. This was the kind of inner reflection that is prompted by something akin to political despair. From this distance it can be hard to remember just how dominant the Blair government was. With more than 400 seats in Parliament, and before the turmoil of the Iraq War, New Labour was in control of the political landscape.

What were the Conservatives to do? Well, according to May, they could start by having a long look at themselves in the mirror. She told the party's annual conference: 'There's a lot we need to do in this party of ours. Our base is too narrow and so, occasionally, are our sympathies. You know what some people call us – the nasty party.' The 'nasty party' tag immediately reverberated inside and outside the party. It was a tag that stuck, a self-inflicted wound that cut deep because it seemed a little too close to the truth. It spoke of a party that needed to modernize its thinking and broaden its base.

That imperative resonated in the thinking of the next generation of the party's MPs. When David Cameron was elected leader in 2005, he looked for ways to 'warm up' his party. He needed to vanquish the 'nasty party' tag by looking for ways to present a socially more progressive form of conservatism. Elected to office as prime minister in 2010, Cameron found an issue capable of projecting the new face of the Conservative Party by deciding to support same-sex marriage. Not only support it, but to lead the fight from the front. The popular perception until that point had been that the Conservatives were reluctant converts, having to be dragged kicking and screaming to legally recognize the rights of the LGBTQ+ community. It had been Labour that had introduced civil partnerships through legislation in 2004, whereas the Tory opposition had been split, without a firm party line on whether to support or oppose the change.

So how do you convince a party built on conservative tradition to adopt a fundamentally progressive social change? The answer for Cameron was that you frame it in conservative language. Instead of focusing his narrative on questions of equality, Cameron focused on the importance of the institution of marriage itself. The traditional institution of marriage was so good, according to Cameron, that absolutely everyone should be free to try it. He was able to tell a conservative story by focusing on the parts of the change that could be framed as a defence of social institutions rather than a challenge to them. As he told the 2011 party conference, 'Yes, it's about equality, but it's also about something else: commitment. Conservatives believe in the ties that bind us; that society is stronger when we make vows to each other and support each other. So I don't support gay marriage despite being a Conservative. I support gay marriage because I am a Conservative.'

The policy problem being addressed here was really about human rights and fundamental equality. But in order to 'sell' his solution to that problem, Cameron constructed a narrative that conservative critics of the change would find it harder to argue against. As Cameron wrote for a piece in the *Daily Mail* in 2013, 'there is something special about marriage . . . the values of marriage are give and take, support and sacrifice – values that we need more of in this country.' What Conservative could disagree with that?

The Marriage (Same Sex Couples) Act passed into law in 2013. It remains a matter of record that many Conservative MPs were not convinced that this was a good idea. A significant number crossed the floor to vote against the bill. At the third reading, 133 Tories went through the 'no' lobby, including ten junior ministers.[2] It was only the overwhelming support from Labour and the Liberal Democrats that ultimately guaranteed the safe passage of the reform through the House of Commons.

But the test for Cameron was not whether he could convince every member of the Tory Party to vote for same-sex marriage. Unanimity on anything in Parliament is unbelievably rare, and even more so when dealing with social reforms of this nature. The challenge for Cameron was whether he could tell a story that was coherent in its narrative, whilst remaining consistent with Conservative Party values as they had traditionally been perceived. Was it possible to build a story convincing enough that large numbers of Conservative MPs could support it without feeling as though they'd undermined their own principles? It was a difficult needle to thread.

Cameron essentially 'redefined' marriage, without actually

changing anything about it. It was a political trick of the light. Instead of drawing the eye to the 'man and woman' component of previous definitions, he focused on the commitment side. That was a political choice which enabled a different narrative, capable of sustaining a conservative case in favour of same-sex marriage. Others, like President Obama in the United States, more squarely framed same-sex marriage as a matter of rights and equality – an equally powerful narrative that resonated comfortably with the more progressive traditions of the Democratic Party.

But when successful reform in the US finally came, it arrived through the Supreme Court adopting a similar narrative about marriage to the one that had brought success for Cameron in England. In writing the majority opinion in the landmark case of *Obergefell v. Hodges*, Justice Kennedy emphasized the traditional underpinnings of marriage, casting the change as a way of strengthening the institution of marriage itself.

> No union is more profound than marriage, for it embodies the highest ideals of love, fidelity, devotion, sacrifice, and family. In forming a marital union, two people become something greater than once they were . . . It would misunderstand these men and women to say they disrespect the idea of marriage. Their plea is that they do respect it, respect it so deeply that they seek to find its fulfillment for themselves.[3]

The importance and power of that narrative is shown by the impact of its absence in other countries. In this same period in the 2010s, prime minister Tony Abbott in Australia had refused to support same-sex marriage by trying to keep the narrative focus there squarely on the 'man and woman' component, positioning marriage as the bulwark that protects traditional family values from what Abbott termed the 'fashion of the moment'. Abbott proved to be wildly out of step with popular sentiment on the issue, including in his own electorate in Sydney. When Australia eventually resolved the issue via a plebiscite in 2017, Abbott's constituents in his seat of Warringah voted 75 per cent in favour of same-sex marriage.

In the UK, Cameron's capacity to build a conservative narrative in favour of same-sex marriage meant that the ructions the issue caused in Australian politics were not experienced in the same way in the UK. It didn't mean that everyone suddenly agreed, but it shaped the politics in favour of reform. It meant that the narrative for change was in alignment with the other aspects, in a party that had traditionally been reticent on the issue. The ducks were able to start swimming.

On 15 December 2010, eyewitnesses described a moment of unspeakable tragedy unfolding before them off the coast of Christmas Island. This Australian external territory, situated between the Australian mainland and Indonesia, had long been a target destination for asylum-seeker boats. On this day, a boat carrying an estimated ninety people or so had reached Christmas Island's wild and rugged coastline. People had made it to within touching distance of the island. But to no avail. Unable to make safe harbour, their boat was smashed, repeatedly, into the coastal cliffs – only metres away from those watching helplessly onshore as people drowned before them.

Each new wave brought fresh catastrophe as people were

thrown into the sea or hurled against the rocks, completely unable to stabilize the vessel in the choppy waters. The confirmed death toll reached forty-eight. The people on board were refugees seeking asylum, mostly from Iraq and Iran. Over weeks and months they had found their way from the Middle East to Indonesia, where they had paid people smugglers to take them on the final dash to Australian territory.

This boat was not the first – nor the last – asylum-seeker vessel to perish on the journey to Australia. But the proximity of the vessel to Christmas Island itself made this a defining moment. People on the island – and Australians watching on their TV screens at home – had been collective witnesses to the tragedy up close. They could see people's faces and their determined struggle for life. They could see children perishing, even as their parents tried desperately to keep them afloat or get them to shore. It was a moment demanding action.

As discussed in the previous chapter, arguments about immigration have been some of the fiercest and most passionately fought policy debates across the Western world since the Second World War. Since the tragic events of 9/11 in the US, those fears have become intertwined with security concerns. Attitudes towards the movement of people have hardened in many countries. Australia has been no exception. Former Prime Minister John Howard won the 2001 election – held only two months after 9/11 – in part by asserting the need to maintain 'control' of Australia's borders. The arrival of asylum-seeker boats at that time was the issue he used to crystallize his 'tough on security' stance. His promise that 'we will decide who comes to this country and the circumstances in which they come' became the dominant rhetorical flourish of the election campaign.

So, when the Christmas Island tragedy unfolded nearly a decade later in December 2010, there was a ready-made, ongoing political debate in play, buttressed by years of argument and dispute on how to treat asylum seekers trying to reach Australia by boat. Both main political parties told a similar story. They would get tough. They would open more offshore processing centres in small Pacific countries, denying 'boat people' the chance to reach Australia at all. A political bidding war developed on just how muscular each party was going to be in taking an uncompromising position on boat arrivals.

In 2010, the Labor Party was experiencing internal ructions as it tried to find an acceptable compromise policy position. Its progressive wing was pushing back against the dehumanizing of asylum seekers in public conversation. Desperate people coming to Australia by boat had been labelled by some on the political right as 'queue jumpers', too impatient to come to Australia by means of more traditional refugee processes. Critics on the left argued that there was in fact no queue to jump, as desperate people fleeing for their lives did not have such formal options available. At the same time, the electoral politics on the issue were hardening. There was a need to at least be seen to be exerting some control. But a coherent narrative able to project *both* strength and compassion remained elusive for the Labor government. The opposition Liberal Party locked onto a much less nuanced storyline. They would 'stop the boats', period. The Liberal leader, Tony Abbott, zeroed in and doubled down with tenacity.

The slogan 'stop the boats' resonated through Australian public life for the next three years of opposition, and then throughout the first term of the Abbott government. It was ubiquitous.

Rather than focus the debate on the victims, Abbott zoned in on the facilitators. The villains of the story here were the people smugglers. These were the people who fleeced refugees of all the money they could muster in return for putting them on overloaded and unseaworthy vessels and sending them towards Australia. They were to be public enemy number one, and like any enemy, what was required was a warlike commitment to routing them out.

In the lead-up to his 2013 election win, Abbott announced that under his prime ministership the country would launch 'Operation Sovereign Borders' in response to this 'national emergency'. A three-star military commander would be put in charge of things. This was storytelling through clear lines and deep symbolism. This was a warlike crisis, and there could be only one goal: 'Stop the boats'. And it was a message that delivered for Abbott. Known for his unrelenting style, this kind of approach played to his strengths. Following his election win on 7 September 2013, he repeated his message: 'The people smugglers are on notice. Their game is up. It's all over for them.'[4]

The range of policy interventions that followed to back up this narrative was consistent in its alignment. The new government had talked tough and the policies it implemented showed a determination to walk that talk. Then Immigration Minister Scott Morrison oversaw the turning around of asylum boats. Some were literally towed back out to sea. Offshore detention was pursued with ever greater resolve, with payments made to Papua New Guinea and Nauru to host Australian immigration detention centres, so that asylum seekers would not be processed on Australian soil. There was evidence of asylum seekers being launched back to Indonesia on specifically designed lifeboats. The government let such allegations swirl without too much overt concern. It suited their political agenda to let such stories run. Abbott himself merely said that Australia was being 'incredibly creative in coming up with a whole range of strategies to break this evil trade'.[5]

There was, of course, an alternative narrative. The United Nations High Commissioner for Refugees criticized the approach of not processing asylum seekers within Australia, and for trying to resettle refugees in poorer countries in the region instead. The UN Special Rapporteur on Torture expressed concern over the detention facilities at the Manus Island site in Papua New Guinea. Abbott would have none of it: 'I really think Australians are sick of being lectured to by the United Nations, particularly, given that we have stopped the boats, and by stopping the boats, we have ended the deaths at sea.'[6]

The government narrative essentially responded to criticisms that the policy was too tough by turning those criticisms on their head and arguing that they were in fact founded in compassion. The *easy* thing to do would be to let deaths at sea continue to happen by keeping the welcome mat out for those seeking a better life in Australia. Only the Liberal government, so the narrative went, had the courage to institute the kind of tough love that would save lives. If that meant towing people back out to sea to get the message across, then so be it.

Whilst the slogan 'stop the boats' claimed the public attention, it was underpinned by a deeper piece of storytelling. A wider narrative about criminal gangs of people smugglers, feeding off the misery of others, ran alongside a security narrative that Australia must be in charge of its borders. It proved a powerful combination. The ducks were indisputably in a row. The government did stop the boats. But that also came at an immense human cost, and amidst significant international criticism of the disregard for the human rights of asylum seekers.

The politics of policymaking can at times seem fiendishly unpredictable, whilst at core remaining surprisingly simple. Governments need to control what they can, and then respond well to what they can't. The rhetorical pulpit that democracy provides for its leaders offers a powerful megaphone through which to define a problem and tell a story about it. The issue of asylum-seeker boats coming to Australia could easily be defined as a humanitarian problem – a test of compassion as people are welcomed into the community whilst they have their asylum-seeker claims assessed.

The Abbott government was determined instead to frame the problem as a national security issue, of the prevention of crime by people smugglers and keeping control of Australia's borders. After 'choosing' that as the problem, the narrative served to drive home the point. The story was about the war on people smugglers. It was relentless. You could tell it was winning the political debate because the Labor Party felt it had no choice but to follow suit. Back in opposition, the party pushed through a policy change in 2015, allowing future Labor governments also to tow boats back out to sea.

In this case, the data and evidence fell into line. It was both quite true and widely reported that the number of boats heading to Australia had increased extensively in the early 2010s. Those wanting to portray this as an 'out-of-control' situation had something to work with. The opposing narrative, highlighting that the vast majority of people who had their status assessed did turn out to be genuine refugees in need of shelter, failed to grip into the debate. The Abbott government, voted into office in 2013, also went to considerable lengths to control the amount of public information released on attempted boat arrivals and the numbers involved. This stopped the political impact of the kind of daily count that had dominated media headlines under the previous government, but also quite rightly drew the ire of transparency campaigners who argued that the public had a right to know what operations the government was carrying out.

But the ducks were in a row, and the government enjoyed considerable support for its hard-line asylum-seeker policies in opinion polls. It had defined the problem in a way that suited its preferred political narrative, and aligned that with interventions that were equally tough. Once more, that does not mean it was the 'right' policy, or the 'best' policy. The international criticisms came thick and fast, and there are harrowing stories of the individual hardship experienced by asylum seekers stuck in offshore detention for years as their cases were assessed. To suggest that the ducks were in a row is not a judgement on the morality of the government's position, but rather an assessment of why they were able to win the politics of policymaking on the issue.

*

Readers of a certain age will remember the emergence in the 1980s of a new kind of literature: the 'choose your own adventure' story. These were heady days. Suddenly the linear act of reading a book turned into a more unpredictable exercise, in which your choices determined the roads that would open before you. The reader waded through the pages in full heroic garb, forced to decide at key moments whether to pick up a sword, question a two-headed snake or run for their lives. Stark choices to make by torchlight at the age of ten, but there you are.

When politicians tell a policy story, they also very often set it out as a personal journey that is populated by stark choices. They are trying to convince the public not to be lured into discussion with strangers (i.e. the opposition!) or to be seduced by the competing narrative on what to do about a policy problem. They purport to be our collective guides in a choose-your-own-adventure tale in which the stakes could hardly be higher.

But they also want to be reassuring. They want to press our emotional triggers whilst convincing us that 'they've got this', as modern parlance would have it. They want to take us to the top of the roller-coaster and invite us to look down and scream, only to then bring us safely back to a stop at the ticket booth. We will be grateful to still be alive, whilst also strangely keen to buy another ticket. In politics, the polling booth takes the place of the ticket booth, but the roller-coaster ride is all too much the same.

To get us to buy a ticket, politicians have to connect with us somehow, convince us that they understand us. How do politicians connect with people? They strive to be authentic, to be 'real', and to show that they have the same problems and foibles as the rest of us. It's an attempt to humanize. And the way to humanize has always been through storytelling. Too often the language of policymaking is vague, bureaucratic, turgid, and indecipherable. It sounds like some kind of conspiracy being perpetrated by elites on ordinary people.[7] Politicians keep it relatable by making it personal – by telling their stories in a way that connects with the policy narrative they are striving to champion.

Because politicians are in the persuasion business, they present narratives as choices in order to ratchet up the clarity of the alternate future that their proposed actions will help avoid. Especially at election time, binary choices are the order of the day. That's where the 'choose your own adventure' comes in. The nuance is dialled down and the tension is dialled up. 'If you elect party X you are voting for higher taxes and lower liberty', they will say. Or, 'If you elect party Y you are voting for the rich to get richer'.

It doesn't necessarily matter if the fates being offered to us are only partly grounded in reality. An element of hyperbole is kind of priced in, as long as the stories resonate and emotionally connect. Stories cut through for all sorts of reasons. The philosopher Aristotle identified three aspects of rhetoric that makes what people say seem persuasive: logos, pathos and ethos. Logos, as its name suggests, is about the logic of the argument. It makes sense. It 'sounds' right.[8] Pathos is actually more about the audience, because it's about trying to build an emotional connection with them through the story that's being told. It takes imagination, with a liberal use of metaphors and imagery to stir the heart and soul of those listening. The third element, ethos, is about the speaker themselves. Do they have a high standing that means you find them trustworthy, authoritative, and authentic?

Some leaders are able to bring all three aspects to the table, whereas others will be stronger on certain elements. When they draw on their personal experience, our leaders are building their ethos through emotional connection. If you hear, for example, that your local member of Congress once lived for six months on the street having been left homeless due to family breakdown, it paints a picture in your head about who they are. If that politician makes a point in debates about homelessness, you're more likely to value their opinion. They have extra authenticity. You will feel (probably quite rightly) as if they know what they're talking about.

The Althing has been in operation for over a millennium. It is the oldest continuing parliamentary institution on earth. Founded in 930 CE, it began as an annual outdoor meeting of the free people of Iceland, who would journey to a place called Þingvellir. The presiding officer would sit on the law rock – the *lögberg* – as new laws were considered and promulgated. Historians can no longer be certain of the exact location of the *lögberg*. What we can be sure about is that when the Althing first gathered in 930, the collection of families and leaders assembled in the rugged landscape would have looked to distant mountains and seen a world of ice. This was a place populated by people experiencing the challenges of life at the farthest edge of the world.

Even today, 10 per cent of Iceland's landmass is made up of glaciers. But in a place like Iceland, the impact of global warming is not something easily hidden. It is written into the landscape because all Iceland's glaciers are in fact in rapid retreat. Like the small, low-lying island countries of the Pacific, for whom rising sea levels are literally an existential threat, Iceland experiences climate change more profoundly than other places. Developing a viable political narrative about climate change is a challenge that Icelandic politicians take seriously. There is storytelling to be done to link the raw data of temperature changes to the kind of human and environmental suffering they result in.

At the 2017 election, one of the many parties in contention for seats was the Left-Green Movement. Their chairperson, Katrín Jakobsdóttir, had been in the Althing since 2007 and had previous ministerial experience as the minister for Education, Science and Culture. But in 2017 she was running for a greater prize. Under Iceland's electoral system (a form of proportional representation), majority governments are unlikely. As in other parts of Scandinavia and northern Europe, government is normally formed by multiple parties hammering out a coalition deal after an election has been held. The Left-Green Movement finished second in the election, winning eleven of the Althing's sixty-three seats. Jakobsdóttir became prime minister in a three-party deal alongside the Independence Party and the Progressive Party. She made it clear from the outset that one of her most important policy goals would be to push forward on addressing climate change.

Like most complex problems, the issue of climate change is composed of a vast interrelated subset of problems that are difficult to solve in one go. In Iceland's case, those problems are intense. As studies have shown, the rate of global warming is greater the closer one lives to the poles. Iceland has already started to see the impacts of global warming as average temperatures rise. The ice is melting. Fishing patterns are changing. So is the island's topography.

As pretty much everyone on planet Earth now knows, carbon emissions into the atmosphere are driving much of the global warming that leads to climate change. All countries contribute to that, and in particular the biggest economies like the USA and China. Iceland is a country of roughly 350,000 people. Even if the whole of Iceland went carbon neutral tomorrow, it would do little to prevent the de-icing of this country, which is responsible for just 0.01 per cent of global carbon emissions.

So what to do? Should politicians just ignore carbon emissions and focus on funding activities that will help to prepare the country for the changes ahead? Successive Icelandic governments have seen that as both morally indefensible and popularly unsustainable. The weather has changed the political conversation, whether politicians like it or not. Climate change is so rapid in Iceland that the locals can see with their own eyes that the glaciers are retreating. It is a simple reality that there is no hiding from.

As prime minister, Katrín Jakobsdóttir told a story about her country's changing environment. Like most powerful stories, it had simple elements underpinning it. The first is to not just acknowledge that there's a problem, but to walk towards it – to embrace it as a reality that needs addressing. The story is one of unavoidable and painful change, linked to a call for action that will help avert the worst whilst adjusting for what is to come.

In 2019, the prime minister wrote an op-ed piece in *The New York Times*, marking the moment that the glacier known as 'Ok' officially ceased being a glacier. Jakobsdóttir went to Ok for the unveiling of a memorial plaque at the site, inscribed with the words: 'Ok is the first Icelandic glacier to lose its status as a glacier. In the next 200 years, all our glaciers are expected to follow the same path. This monument is to acknowledge that we know what is happening and what needs to be done. Only you know if we did it.'

It's a powerful message. But there are also two other notable elements to it. The first is its title: it's called 'A Letter to the Future'. The second is that beneath the inscription there are some numbers. There, etched into history, is the carbon reading in parts per million of 415 p.p.m. CO_2 – the record atmospheric CO_2 reading recorded in 2019.

The plaque is in fact a collaboration between scientists and Icelanders, and not simply a piece of government messaging. But it nonetheless provides a powerful start for a narrative about what is happening and what needs to change. It amplifies the need to do this, not just for this generation, but for future generations. And it records for posterity a particular piece of data – the p.p.m. reading – that helps to make the story real. It gets the ducks in a row.

In her op-ed piece, Jakobsdóttir summed it up beautifully: 'The ice is leaving Iceland.'

This line is a five-word story in itself. It has emotion, pathos. The ice is presented as something magical to which we are waving a sad goodbye. But the melancholy is not left to overwhelm us because there is more to the story. Action is being taken to encourage the magic to stay with us. 'As the prime minister of Iceland, I am determined that my government will play its part. We are currently executing Iceland's first fully funded action plan, aiming at carbon neutrality by 2040 at the latest. Iceland has decarbonized energy production, and we are working toward greener transport, including by proposing a ban on the registration of cars powered by non-renewables after 2030.'

What this does is break down a seemingly impossible task into smaller component parts. It explains that there are very specific things that can be done to bring down CO_2 emissions: moving to renewable energy, changing the way cars are powered, setting overall carbon-neutrality goals. It ensures that we have a fuller story. A cast of characters, with a specific goal in mind, and all sorts of hell to go through in order to get there.

Let's pause for a moment and consider a literary and movie classic like *The Lord of the Rings*. Now here is a story for the ages. A tale of good and evil and the overcoming of seemingly insurmountable odds. Frodo is safely tucked up in the Shire, blissfully unperturbed by the outside world. Yet the dangers of that world find him nonetheless. A menace hangs over the land and he must do his part to fight it, however small and powerless he might feel. His friends are an essential ingredient of the story, for without them success is not possible. It must be a communal effort, a shared act of bravery. At the apex of the story in the movie version, as the hobbit Pippin looks down from the ramparts of Minas Tirith, awaiting the next move of the forces of darkness, he confides to Gandalf: 'I don't want to be in a battle. But waiting on the edge of one I can't escape is even worse.'

Now, ask yourself, is the Icelandic saga of climate change really much different? There is an existential threat hanging over a land that once sat quietly on the edge of the world, unbothered by the rumbles of the great powers. To meet that threat, the Icelanders must look outwards and forge a coalition of the willing, urging other countries to join them in the fight, through organizations like the Arctic Council and the United Nations. The battle has been joined. Just as the exhausted soldiers of Gondor looked to the horizon to see if Rohan would come to their aid, so too are small nations like Iceland casting their eyes outward to see who will help them. As the rising temperatures come to take the ice from Iceland, its political leaders say no, there is still hope and still time to act.

It is of course – at one level – quite fanciful. I am not suggesting that the solution to climate change is to throw the 'one ring' into a glacial lake and hope it refreezes. But it shows how political storytelling is an absolutely integral part of policymaking. Just throwing facts at people and then putting a policy intervention in place doesn't cut it. The story provides the fuel for action. It puts the problem and the evidence about it into a form that is more easily consumable. It connects the change – to electric cars for instance – to a wider story in which we can play our part.

Our political leaders are telling us policy stories all the time, even when we don't realize it. Sometimes even they don't realize it! The challenge is to be able to tell a persuasive story, even in the face of considerable opposition to a policy idea. Political instincts are great for telling stories that are going with the flow of public opinion, but statecraft can sometimes require the opposite. It takes skill, resilience and determination to tell a story that takes the public with you in the face of their own reservations.

Skill, resilience and determination are characteristics that former German Chancellor Angela Merkel possesses in spades. Very few democratic leaders anywhere on the globe have managed to stay in office for sixteen years. Fewer still have then left office with their popularity still broadly intact. Merkel managed both, despite having to lead Germany through some of the major upheavals of the twenty-first century – the 2008 financial crisis, the migrant crisis, and the Covid pandemic, to name just three.

In 2015, the civil war in Syria had been under way for four long years. The scale of human suffering was immense. Millions of people were internally displaced as families found themselves surrounded by a conflict they could not control. The forces of Bashar al-Assad, leader of the Syrian Arab Republic, clashed with a range of opposition groups in different parts of the country. Amidst the mayhem, the ISIL (Islamic State of Iraq and the Levant) group gained control of a vast swathe of territory spreading across eastern Syria and northern Iraq, forcing many more families to flee.

The result was a refugee tide of misery as displaced people fled the war zones. The direction of that tide was towards Europe. The story is a complex one, as EU countries in eastern Europe and the Mediterranean saw hundreds of thousands of people come to and through their borders. The pathways through which people could travel were in a state of flux as some countries closed their borders altogether, forcing asylum seekers onwards via different routes. In total, well over a million refugees came to Europe's door in the course of 2015.

Public opinion within the EU, and within its constituent countries, was divided on what should be done. There was a noticeable hardening of opinion on the right, with the government in Hungary under Viktor Orbán receiving strong domestic support for refusing to take in large numbers, and parties like the Alternative für Deutschland (Alternative for Germany, or AfD) seeing their stocks rise in Germany as they spoke out against the country taking in large numbers of refugees. But with hundreds of thousands of asylum seekers stuck at border points across the south and east of Europe, something needed to give. Angela Merkel, highlighting Germany's heightened responsibility as a leader within the EU, stepped forward.

It was not a conventional policy process, if such a thing even exists. This was policymaking in crisis, under pressure from international events. Merkel chose to define the problem sympathetically, as a humanitarian crisis for which those fleeing towards Europe could not be held responsible. There was little doubt that the majority of the refugees were genuinely on the run from armed conflict. The desperate situation in Syria and Iraq had been well documented by the world's media for years.

The extent of the problem was overwhelming. It could not be ignored, but nor could it be controlled in any kind of 'normal' process. In one of the boldest policy interventions of her tenure, Merkel decided that Germany had to throw open its own borders and accept the majority of the refugees itself. The political bravery involved in that decision should not be underestimated. As leader of a centre-right party, Merkel was well aware that elements in the Christian

Democratic Union (CDU) itself were very uncomfortable with her stance. Success was not guaranteed, and the potential for electoral backlash was immense. But having defined a problem and decided on a course of action, the final piece of the puzzle was the narrative. Merkel had to find a form of words to explain to the German people, and a wider constituency within the EU, why this was the right course of action.

Her approach was well encapsulated in her speech to the CDU party conference in December 2015. Merkel told a story that resonated with a deep understanding of German history and the German psyche. It was a story that appealed to the head with its economic arguments, and to the heart with its humanitarian dimensions. The ballast came from the moral undertone about Germany's unique historical responsibility to be a place which welcomes those displaced by war. 'The CDU is a party that from the beginning knew that after the horror of the Second World War and the Holocaust, our Germany could only come back to its feet politically and morally if we overcame separations and built bridges beyond the borders of our own country'.[9]

It was a powerful story. But that's not to say it was an easy sell, or that everyone was convinced. In some ways, that's not the point. The narrative was strong enough, clear enough, and nuanced enough to make sure it aligned with both the problem and the policy, but in such a way as to give Merkel a fighting chance politically. It was strong on the responsibility to accept refugees, but equally strong on what would then be expected of them. 'Whoever seeks refuge with us needs to respect our laws, values and traditions'.[10] She indicated that refugee numbers would need to fall significantly in the future, and that other European countries also needed to step up and do their share.

Her speech to the CDU was a masterclass in political rhetoric, combining logical explanation with emotional connection, bringing her party back together after a difficult year grappling with the refugee issue. The ducks were in a row and swimming hard. What united them most of all was Merkel herself. Few leaders could have mustered the political capital that had allowed her to survive the challenges of 2015 with her authority intact. It was the respect for her – even affection – that gave the story power. Her ethos underpinned the power of her appeal.

The moral is that stories matter, but so too does the storyteller. The connection between the two must demonstrate an underlying authenticity in order to be fully effective. If that can be linked to a clearly articulated problem, then the battle is already half won, and the first two ducks are in a row. But, as the next chapter explains, what can still go wrong is that the underpinnings of the story can fall away when subjected to greater scrutiny. In other words, the 'facts' – the hard evidence about what is really going on – can cause a carefully woven tale to unravel in alarming ways.

3. Getting the Facts Straight

In the Middle Ages, the clans of the west coast of Scotland used the sea very much as the highways of their day. Small boats, known in Gaelic as *bìrlinn*, sailed and rowed their way in and out of the island waters from the Hebrides to the Argyll peninsula. Multipurpose by design, these craft could serve not only as a way of moving people and exerting military power, but also as fishing and trading vehicles. Known in English as a West Highland galley, these nifty vessels were perfect for navigating both along the coast and also in the narrower waterways and channels that dominate the Scottish shoreline. With a shallow draught, they could land easily and quickly in most places.

West Highland galleys are symbols of a bygone age, but also capture something of the romance of the Highlands and islands. Nature seems closer there; the air crisper, the whisky smokier and the fish fresher. This gives Scotland a unique marketing advantage in the realm of natural produce. In a world of mass production of foodstuffs, Scotland seems to offer something unique; something infused with the air and the wild fresh waters of the Atlantic. It is a form of magic that sells. Fresh food from Scotland is a sought-after commodity that can command premium prices in the market halls of Europe.

The distribution of these natural wonders no longer relies on the steady hull of a *birlinn* for transport. These days even such zippy vessels are not fast enough to meet modern demands. Scotland's foodstuffs are transported by air, at speed, to reach the shops and stores of Europe within twenty-four hours of being harvested. They have to be. This speed is what guarantees their freshness, which is the signature mark of the quality these products are known for. Disrupt that speed and, commercially, things quickly start to go wrong.

That is exactly what happened in the opening days of 2021. As the Covid pandemic ravaged the UK's physical and economic health, something else ravaged the export of Scottish seafood to the continent. The impact was immediate and economically devastating. Fish were literally left rotting on the docks, or in warehouses, unable to make the short journey from Scotland to the shops of France, Netherlands, and Germany in time. The alleged culprit identified was a well-known evil that governments had long promised to vanquish: bureaucratic red tape.

What had unleashed this latest barrage of paperwork was the decision made by the sovereign government of the United Kingdom to relinquish the country's membership of the European Union. In a word, Brexit. The EU, of course, has a common market. Goods and services can flow freely between European countries, without the restrictions imposed by normal international borders. From 1 January 2021, this no longer applied to the UK. Having officially left the EU a year earlier, and having arrived at the end of the year-long transition period, change suddenly became very real.

Inspections, regulations, border paperwork and other

restrictions now applied to British seafood exporters trying to get their produce into the EU. What had previously been achievable in less than a day was suddenly taking many days. The fish that had been fresh when it left Scottish shores was going rotten by the time it showed up in Boulogne. Unsaleable, this valuable cargo simply had to be dumped.

How could such a dramatic and devastating impact have been allowed to occur? Couldn't someone have warned the government that the British economy was so intertwined with that of the EU that Brexit would result in such challenges? Well, yes . . . many, many such warnings were made. Not just by the governments of the EU, but also by the Remain side in the UK referendum of 2016. For months during that referendum campaign, politicians, campaigners, industry groups and 'experts' had been pouring data into the public domain that gave testament to the likelihood that Brexit would involve a huge economic shock to the UK. They could point to modelling that predicted a certain number of businesses would go bust, and a set number of percentage points would have to be deducted from GDP (Gross Domestic Product) over the next few decades as a result of Brexit. The warnings over the regulation of trade to the EU, including for the export of fresh produce, came in waves.

Despite this, many fishing communities and their industry associations had in fact been strongly in the pro-Brexit 'Leave' camp. How could this be? How could such a mass of hard data and evidence fail to convince even this group of people that leaving the EU would be an economically damaging idea?

The reason is at one level quite simple. It's because data and evidence don't speak for themselves. Without interpretation, they are just numbers or words on a page. The Remain campaign failed because it forgot simple truths about how politics works. It did not get its ducks in a row. It had the evidence, but no story to make it sing, no narrative to stir the hearts and minds of the very voters who would find themselves in the greatest danger from Brexit impacts. On the Leave side, the Brexiteers were able to paint a compelling picture of a problem that needed to be solved. They told a story about British identity that had real emotional appeal, and pointed to the clearest of all possible interventions as the way to fix things: to 'simply' leave the EU. The weakest of the ducks for the Leave camp was the data and evidence. Their claims were the more speculative. The economic data were so often against them. Few would now forget the exaggerated flourish of the messages promising that hundreds of millions of pounds would be reallocated to the NHS once the money was safely reclaimed from the allegedly wasteful hands of the Europeans.

It didn't matter. The pro-Brexit camp had the positive story to tell. The data duck might have been swimming weakly, but the other three of the four ducks dragged it along. There was an intrinsic understanding of the emotional foundations that were driving Brexit forward. Not least among Britain's fishing communities. For four decades, British fishers had been forced to share their waters with the fishing fleets of other EU nations. Fishing on a vast scale threatened the viability of some fisheries. For them, a policy that promised to 'take back control' had a very real resonance. That resonance was more powerful than warnings that there might be an economic price to pay in other ways.

And there was no shortage of data, both before and after

the referendum, suggesting that disruption was highly likely. Government statistics showed that 80 per cent of British wild-caught seafood went to export in 2015, and overwhelmingly to the EU.[1] An OECD paper on the Economic Consequences of Brexit warned of 'higher administrative costs related to customs controls'.[2] Warnings that fish could be left to rot on the docks were dismissed as 'a load of old tosh' by some British fishers.[3]

The Institute for Government is an independent think tank in London, respected by all the UK's major political parties. Following the referendum, it published a series of papers on the challenges Brexit would bring. Amongst them was customs disruption. 'Traders who are used to moving goods freely to the EU will need to adapt. They will have new requirements for paperwork and their goods could face significant checks at the EU border. Supply chains that are optimized for speed and fluidity will need to find the space and time for customs authorities to carry out checks and inspections.'[4]

The moral of the story is that data and evidence by themselves can achieve very little. In fact, the Remain side seemed to have nothing going for it *except* the data and evidence. There was no clear 'problem', because they were quite happy with the way things were. But there was also no clear story for why the UK should stay in Europe either. There was plenty of data showing it would be economically better off, but no emotional connection to what that would mean. There was no narrative about the miracle of the EU, which in the space of a few decades had bound together a continent twice ripped asunder by world war and turned it into a peaceful economic powerhouse. There was no clear set of interventions for how to fix grievances that could match the compelling finality of the policy put forward by the Brexiteers: to simply leave the EU.

We like to think that 'the facts' about any issue are self-explanatory; that they 'speak for themselves'. Not so. Data do not have communicative powers. Evidence never buys a round of drinks. Facts always rely on interpretation. A graph is just lines on a piece of paper until someone chooses to build it into a story that the rest of us can understand. But the same applies in reverse. Without the data and evidence to underpin it, a narrative is just a fairy tale in danger of being mugged by the facts. Accurate information remains at the very heart of the policy process. Despite contemporary concerns about political spin, fake news and post-truth, even the most political of policy messages will eventually flounder without some evidential support.

The difficulty is that we never actually know the full truth about anything. Politics and policy are trapped in the 'bounded rationality' that I mentioned earlier.[5] That means that all the data and evidence that underpins policymaking is of necessity imperfect and selective. This makes decision-making harder. There is almost never a universal view on which way the data are pointing. From climate change to Covid, there are always some scientific experts who will provide a different reading of the evidence. That is what allows politicians themselves the room to frame an issue by selecting those pieces of evidence that most support their own preferred version of events.

This does not mean that politicians can simply ignore the evidence altogether without consequences. The public record is replete with instances where the overwhelming weight of the evidence has overturned a preferred political narrative. Failure to align the evidence with the other factors means the ducks are not in a row. That's what Tony Blair and George W. Bush found when pointing to weapons of mass destruction that did not materialize. It's also what happened in the UK's exams fiasco. The evidence has a tendency of coming back to bite.

The extraordinary tragedy of Covid-19 proved to be the most universally harrowing health, economic, and social emergency the world has faced for decades. The toll in human suffering is incalculable. The economic and social impacts are continuing to play out.

What is remarkable from a public policy point of view is the sheer weight of data and evidence that has poured into the public domain. Around the globe, once almost unknown government scientists and medical officers became household names. Anthony Fauci, then the head of the National Institute of Allergy and Infectious Diseases, reached celebrity status in the USA. His every utterance was parsed for medical insight, and to see whether he would contradict President Trump's own pronouncements on the pandemic. In the UK, novelty mugs of Chief Medical Officer Sir Chris Whitty became must-have Christmas gifts following his almost daily appearances alongside the prime minister at Downing Street briefings.[6] In Australia, then Chief Medical Officer Dr Brendan Murphy was equally ubiquitous, alongside scientific advisers from state governments.

And these scientists did not come empty-handed. They

came with charts, statistics, data and evidence in tow. *En masse*. Alongside the novelty mugs, T-shirts emerged of Sir Chris Whitty's face beside the words: 'Next slide please'. The slides in question were the graphs he showed at his briefings, plotting the rise and fall of Covid infections, and the likely trajectory of the pandemic in months ahead. There was a worldwide hunger for such information. Governments were desperate to show that they were 'following the data' and being 'led by the science'.

But evidence is complicated stuff. Politicians love clear, clean-cut messages because they know that's what the voters want. Scientists, on the other hand, recognize complexity as inherent to their work. They know that every piece of information and advice comes with caveats, margins of error, and modelling parameters. It's laudably accurate, but politically inconvenient. Throughout the pandemic, governments were falling over themselves to show that they had things under control. They each created a rhetorical frame, a story, about the approach they were taking and why they were taking it. In the early stages of the pandemic, some of those stories got overtaken by the facts. Where the data and evidence didn't align, voters lost faith. Decisive leadership only works if the evidence holds up. King Canute announcing he is holding back the tide is less convincing if he's being swept out to sea. The truth, of course, is that Canute was actually trying to demonstrate that kings were not gods who could hold back the waves. It was a lesson lost on many twenty-first century governments, who were all too willing to pretend that Covid could be dissipated by their command alone.

The Covid-19 pandemic crisis was a real-time experiment

in governance, as well as a real-time human tragedy. Politicians across the world tried to chart their way through 'the science', to make the data and evidence work in their favour. But what was the evidence actually showing? The government of each country took markedly different approaches, based on the data that they were presented with and how that could be mixed with their preferred political narratives. To draw that out, let's take a look at the data which confronted the Swedish government, the New Zealand government and the Brazilian government in the first half of 2020 when Covid hit, and discuss how they fared. This tale of three countries shows much about data and evidence, but also what happens when it runs into politics.

Sweden

'Sweden was right'. That was the judgement shared by Tesla founder Elon Musk with his 54 million Twitter followers on 10 October 2020. He was not alone in drawing that conclusion. It mirrored a widespread belief amongst supporters of Sweden's approach to the pandemic that it had managed to find the right balance between protecting public health and allowing normal life to continue with a minimum of restrictions. And for most of 2020, the data and evidence seemed to provide grounds for a positive conclusion. It backed up the government narrative that Sweden could do things differently whilst still being 'science-led'.

Like other countries, Sweden too found a public face that could exude scientific competence on behalf of government.

Anders Tegnell, with the somewhat forbidding title of state epidemiologist, gave daily briefings as part of the response. Due to Sweden's unique insistence that the pandemic could be addressed without compulsory lockdowns, Tegnell also became a subject of fascination for worldwide media keen to understand the basis of the Swedish approach. In April 2020 he gave an interview to the journal *Nature*, emphasizing the importance of Sweden's tradition of 'individual responsibility' that places the onus on citizens to take steps not to spread communicable diseases. He was at pains to stress that there was – at that point – not much science to follow. 'It is difficult to talk about the scientific basis of a strategy with these types of disease, because we do not know much about it and we are learning as we are doing, day by day. Closedown, lockdown, closing borders — nothing has a historical scientific basis, in my view.'[7]

He emphasized the different governmental tradition in Sweden, which placed high trust in the common sense of the Swedish people. 'As a society, we are more into nudging: continuously reminding people to use measures, improving measures where we see day by day that they need to be adjusted.' But that did not mean that things were not being driven by data and evidence. Tegnell emphasized the 'detailed modelling', daily data analysis, and statistical tracking that accompanied the Swedish strategy.

And the overall data for much of 2020 seemed to make Sweden's approach at least defensible. In the harshest months of the first wave – April and May 2020 – Sweden sometimes suffered hundreds of deaths per week, but so did most European countries. As many readers will remember all too vividly, the initial European wave crashed first into Italy and Spain, reaching Scandinavia more slowly. On 31 March, for example, confirmed cases per million people were running at 171 per day in Spain, 34.5 in Sweden and 31 in Denmark. By 30 June 2020, things had changed. Sweden was then recording 97 cases per million people per day, compared to just eight in Spain and five in Denmark.[8] The numbers kept changing dramatically in all three countries as the first wave receded, and then the second wave began.

What about the economic difference? Part of the appeal of the Swedish model was that it might buffer the economic hit from the virus by keeping businesses like restaurants open and trading. The numbers show that Sweden certainly did better than larger economies like Spain and the UK in the second quarter of 2020. It suffered an economic hit of 8.3 per cent on GDP that quarter compared to the year before. The UK by comparison was down 21.7 per cent. But Denmark was also down less at 'only' 8.5 per cent, whilst also recording a much, much lower death rate than Sweden (107 deaths per million compared with Sweden's 573).[9] So whilst Sweden did better than many European countries, the different Covid compliance settings did not provide an outsized economic benefit compared to its nearest neighbours.

Covering the whole of 2020, statistics suggest that Sweden suffered an excess death rate 7.7 per cent higher than average – i.e. 7.7 per cent more people died than would die in a 'normal' year. That seemingly compares well with Spain at 18.1 per cent. But it compares less favourably with other Scandinavian countries, with Denmark's figure being 1.5 per cent and Norway's zero.[10] Nonetheless, for much of 2020,

Sweden could at least argue that it was doing reasonably well, without having to sacrifice its more liberal approach. It had a narrative that was not immediately in conflict with the data. The two swam in alignment.

But, as so much of the world has found out, pandemics do not stand still. Data can change and overwhelm a political narrative in a matter of weeks. Juxtaposing Sweden's experience against that of the UK is instructive. In the UK, the British government suffered intense criticism for much of 2020 for being slow into lockdown, providing inadequate supplies of PPE, and seeing some of the highest Covid death rates by population in the world. That woeful health outcome was combined with an equally woeful economic performance, as the UK suffered the biggest fall in GDP amongst the G7 countries. The government's refrain that it was building a world-class test-and-trace system and that PPE shortages were being addressed simply did not match with what people were experiencing on the ground. Opinion polls showed alarming distrust of the government approach, and the steady-handed new opposition leader Keir Starmer was rising high in the polls simply for exuding competence.

Yet in 2021, the 'facts' suddenly caught up with the government's preferred narrative as the success of the vaccination programme became apparent. A government approach that had looked unsure at best and incompetent at worst, suddenly turned around. The vaccination campaign proved to be stunningly successful, with high initial take-up rates seeing the UK surging ahead of a struggling EU. The USA exhibited a similar turnaround. In Sweden, the opposite was suddenly true. The calm, measured approach which had eschewed lockdowns was shaken by a second wave of infections which came crashing into Sweden's health system in the final weeks of 2020 and early 2021. High levels of public trust began to erode rapidly. Polling by IPSOS found that 'confidence is in a downward spiral'[11] as deaths climbed dramatically by comparison to neighbouring countries, which had all adopted formal lockdowns at various points. Sweden's King Carl XVI Gustaf declared in an interview: 'I think we have failed'.[12]

The example demonstrates the importance of the link between the evidence and the story being told about it. When these were working in alignment, Sweden's government looked as if it had discovered the magic formula. It could tell a story about Swedish liberalism and the good sense of the Swedish people that matched with statistics showing a balance between health impacts and economic ones. Sweden was beating Covid in a very 'Swedish' way. It was following the science without being enslaved by it. That story had to change when the data underpinning it started to crumble. In late 2020 and early 2021, the facts refused to support the preferred narrative any longer. Covid fought back.

New Zealand

Sometimes in life, we just need a drink. The idea that we can grab a glass of wine or a beer at the end of a tough working week and try and unwind is baked into cultures across the Western world. We all know it's not particularly healthy. Medical associations frequently and quite rightly point out the negative impacts of alcohol. And yet, we persist. It's our right to have a drink and that's all there is to it. Sadly, this seems to be even more the case when we are away from home. An overnight stay in a hotel, without the difficulty of needing to drive anywhere afterwards, makes the allure of a drink even greater.

To fulfil our desire for alcohol, we might pop down to the hotel bar, or maybe just wander down to the nearest liquor store and grab what we want. It's an easy convenience. But in July 2020, one New Zealander was arrested for doing just that. He wasn't staying in any ordinary hotel, though; to head to the liquor store, he'd literally had to cut his way out of his accommodation. He was in a government quarantine hotel on New Zealand's North Island. Having headed back home from Australia at short notice to deal with a family emergency, he was enduring the frustration of having to stay in his hotel room for two weeks. One week in, he went out to search for alcohol, and instead found himself under arrest. He was not alone in trying to escape from his quarantine quarters. In Auckland, another man absconded to head to a local supermarket. Elsewhere, a woman jumped a hedge and promptly got lost, needing police help to find her way back.

The New Zealand government approach to quarantine got tough after a minor blunder a few weeks earlier had led to some major complications. In June 2020, two British women who had flown into New Zealand had been allowed to leave quarantine without being tested. Released on compassionate grounds, they had borrowed a car from friends to drive 400 miles to visit a dying relative. Unbeknownst to them, they were also carrying Covid. Their symptoms began to appear as they progressed into their car journey. The New Zealand health authorities had to play catch-up, in the face of significant media alarm that this had been allowed to happen. They scrambled to test all possible people who might have come into contact with the women on their journey. The government also set its jaw against any more compassionate exemptions. Symbolically, what do you do if you want to send out a message that you're getting tough? You call in the military, of course. That's exactly what the New Zealand government did, handing over responsibility for quarantine operations to the military to make sure people would not again try to leave ahead of time and without being tested.

Such examples serve to highlight just how extraordinary recent times have been. The Covid pandemic forced governments and citizens to confront restrictions and challenges previously unheard of. Limitations that were once unthinkable became the norm. If you'd told someone in 2019 that the next year they would not be allowed to travel freely to see dying relatives, or help out their family in an emergency, they would have been floored. If you'd said that this would happen not by accident but by government decree, they would have started laughing and waving copies of *1984* by George Orwell in your face. If you'd said that these actions would also win overwhelming popular support, they would surely have shaken their head in disbelief. That's the Covid story. And it's not just a New Zealand story. It's a story repeated across the globe, as country after country struggled to find the right way to respond. But there were a few things in particular that New Zealand managed to get right in those crucial months in 2020.

There are some natural advantages that accrue to being a set of small islands at the far end of the world. One is that there is relatively low through-traffic. When a global pandemic hits, a quick-acting government can still hope to have some chance of shutting the front door in time. Once governments in Europe finally realized the full extent of what was befalling them as the first wave descended, it was already too late. The sheer movement of people through regional transit hubs, and intra-EU holidaymakers, made full suppression of the virus an unrealistic prospect for EU countries.

Not so for New Zealand. It still had a chance. Not for nothing was it identified in university research in 2021 as one of the best places on the planet to withstand a total global meltdown.[13] But New Zealand didn't decide to just ride its geographic luck. Rather, from the outset, it got its ducks in a row. It started with a clear problem definition. The problem was twofold but blindingly clear: keep Covid from getting in; and if any did get in, jump on it with full force. This aligned with the data and evidence, which was clearly and transparently shared as it became available. The political narratives that accompanied it managed to combine positivity with pragmatism. The country was rhetorically drawn together by Prime Minister Jacinda Ardern as 'Team New Zealand', with every player exhorted to do their part to stop the spread of the virus. People were told to act in public as though they had the virus, to make sure its spread was minimized. Ministers were to act as role models, and when several didn't follow the guidance they were swiftly dealt with.

New Zealand's first recorded case of Covid occurred in late February 2020. It made the country the forty-eighth to have declared a confirmed case at the time.[14] Like most countries during the first wave, what followed was a surge of cases in

March. According to World Health Organization figures, there were 410 confirmed cases by 23 March 2020.[15] By 20 April, this was back down to twenty-three confirmed cases, as lockdowns and restrictions started to bite. As of 23 May 2021, New Zealand had recorded twenty-six deaths attributed to Covid, and a total of 2,306 confirmed cases. To put that in perspective, in May 2021, the UK was regularly recording over 2,000 new cases *every day*, and this was considered such outstandingly *good* news that restrictions could be lifted rather than imposed. Even allowing for the UK's vastly larger population, the comparison remains stark.

The government's story was that a committed, cohesive, community-wide approach to eliminate Covid, rather than simply to minimize it, was possible. Few countries in the world at the time agreed. The data proved otherwise. At least for a while, New Zealand became a global success story, the little country that stared down the goliath pandemic that had ravaged all else in its path. The Ardern government was rewarded at a general election in October 2020 with overwhelming support, increasing its vote share dramatically and achieving majority government – no easy feat under the country's proportional electoral system.

In a reminder that politics is fluid, the certainties of 2020 were replaced in 2021 by renewed challenge as the Delta variant found its way into Auckland. In August 2021, Prime Minister Ardern announced a full, tight national lockdown after the discovery of a single case. This was accompanied by criticism that going for an elimination strategy was no longer realistic or valid, as the number of infections extended into the hundreds in the space of only a week. There had also been criticism of New Zealand's slow vaccination roll-out compared to the UK and the USA. Such is the relationship between politics and policymaking. It is iterative. It never sits still. Narratives only hold whilst the data supports them. But what followed in 2021 does not change the fact that for much of 2020, New Zealand was one of the few governments in the world that could rightly claim to have had its ducks in a row.

Brazil

When someone dies at the age of forty-two it shocks us. Death is tragic at all ages, of course, but expectations of reasonable life expectancy help define what we think of as 'enough'. Our sense of tragedy has a keener edge when a young child dies than when a great-grandparent passes away, even if the feelings of grief are intense in either case. When Paulo Gustavo died from Covid in Brazil at the age of forty-two, it shocked the whole country. As an event, it provided stark evidence of what this dreadful disease could do. If it could take a fit and healthy man in the prime of his life, then surely it could take anyone.

Gustavo had been one of Brazil's most famous actors. A comedian, he inhabited the iconic role of Dona Hermínia, a mother humorously dealing with the fact that her son is gay.[16] At forty-two, he was in his prime in pretty much every way. But when Covid caught him, it did so mercilessly. He spent over a month in intensive care before finally succumbing to the virus. His tragic, untimely death was just one exemplar amongst the hundreds of thousands of Brazilians to die at the hands of Covid. Such was his fame that even President Bolsonaro marked his passing.

Throughout much of the pandemic, Bolsonaro's words had been focused not on the virus, but on Brazil's need to simply press on as normal without allowing Covid to knock the country's economy off course. Political rhetoric is a powerful thing. What politicians say matters. Their words and phrases provide the leadership that citizens respond to. Democratic leaders are given a stage with a guaranteed audience. Unlike actors in the cinema, the audience will keep tuning in, even if they think the performance being given is unpersuasive. If a president has something to say, there will be people there to listen. And throughout the pandemic, President Bolsonaro had plenty to say. He treated the virus like another opponent that he could somehow debate. He belittled it. He dismissed its importance and its power. When he himself caught the virus, he strove to laugh it off as though it were little more than a common cold. His core, consistent message to Brazilians was that this disease was neither as important nor as powerful as reporting from the rest of the world seemed to suggest.

This powerful narrative of defiance ran into difficulty when it was progressively overwhelmed by the facts. The data and evidence simply would not support the story being told. No amount of insistence that everything was fine could overcome the demonstrable reality that it wasn't. By August 2021, Brazil had recorded over 20 million coronavirus cases. Over 570,000 people had died from Covid, the second highest total in absolute terms in the world.[17] Vaccination rates had been slow, and the health system in poorer parts of the country had been brought to its knees. To make matters worse, Brazil also saw a new and potentially more dangerous and contagious variant of the virus emerge.

Bolsonaro had been adamant from the start that the disease must take second place to the health of the Brazilian economy. He was initially dismissive of mask-wearing and social distancing. He questioned the need for vaccines and refused to support state governors wanting to pursue a more inter-ventionist public health approach. Some critiques have characterized his approach as an example of 'necropolitics' – the politics of life and death.[18] In November 2020, Bolsonaro declared that 'all of us are going to die one day . . . we have to stop being a country of sissies'.[19]

Bolsonaro's rhetorical journey through the pandemic reflects the relationship between the narrative and the data. He began by simply dismissing the virus's power. The implication was that healthy people would simply be able to shake it off, something Bolsonaro strove to show by example when he caught it himself. Making the pandemic seem like no big deal would withdraw its power to frighten the Brazilian people. Very quickly, as the first wave tore through the country, the evidence tore down that narrative. Too many people could see the impact with their own eyes, as thousands died and intensive care wards filled up.

That left Bolsonaro with a political challenge. He needed to somehow shift the narrative back into alignment to get his ducks in a row. He could have done that by acknowledging the seriousness of the virus and ramping up the policy support for combating it. Instead, he tried a different tack. He essen-tially shrugged his philosophical shoulders. Rather than downplaying the obvious fact that Covid was killing Brazilians, he pivoted to saying that death was a fact of life. Yes, the virus was having serious consequences, but there was no point in railing against it. It was quite a breathtaking way of momentarily getting the narrative and the data back in alignment. The reason it couldn't work politically was because the problem itself had not gone away. An esoteric argument about life and death is hard to sustain when hospitals are running out of beds and thousands of people a day are dying.

A look across the government responses in Sweden, New Zealand and Brazil reveals three different ways in which governments tried to integrate the data and evidence on coronavirus into a particular perception of political reality. Different levels of government intervention, varying narratives on whether and why it was necessary to intervene at all, but all faced with the stark reality of statistics that could not be spun out of the way. The data could not be filibustered into submission, and attempts to fit it into preferred political frames came crashing into the tragic reality of people dying.

Two points hold true. The first is that voters aren't stupid. Governments who attempt to gaslight their own populations will ultimately get found out. Data and evidence matter. Without them, political narratives eventually collapse under the weight of their own surrealism. I'm not saying spin doesn't work or isn't important – of course it is. There is a good reason why governments are obsessed with framing the stories they put out. But stories don't exist in an alternate universe. Politicians who insist the earth is flat will eventually fall off.

The second is that ducks swim – they don't just sit still. The four components need to keep up with each other if they are to stay in alignment. What might have been a popular policy yesterday, based solidly on the evidence, may tomorrow find itself a discredited mess that has been overtaken by a different reality. Strict lockdown policies in New Zealand were justified whilst elimination of the virus was a reasonable possibility. When that changed, the narrative and the problem definition needed to change with it. In Sweden, the exact reverse was true. A narrative about balance and individual liberty could only hold as long as the health side of the scales didn't tip too alarmingly. Once the virus slipped its leash in the second wave, the narrative came under intense pressure along with it. In Brazil, the president's narrative and policy choices were in alignment from the outset, but they simply proved unpalatable when the reality of Covid deaths came knocking. No rhetoric was capable of keeping it out.

Evidence can be inconvenient, and not just in Covid cases. The politics of policymaking sees governments trying to balance so many things. Fundamentals like jobs and the economy are never far away from the centre of political debate. But that doesn't make them easy topics to discuss. For example, how do you tell communities that relied on old industries that their jobs have gone and won't be back in the same form? Old industrial heartlands in the UK, USA and elsewhere have shown what can happen if political leaders don't at least try to save jobs and livelihoods. Governments rely on being able to inspire optimism when communities are facing economic setbacks. But sometimes this can result in patently absurd attempts to spin the evidence in unsustainable ways. The evidence has a habit of fighting back.

Many readers will remember a rather wonderful story from 2016, as Britain sought a new name for a polar research ship that was about to be launched. What do you do in our integrated age when looking to build popularity and exposure for the naming of something? The answer of course is to ask the internet. Sometimes the great democratic leveller and champion of worldwide debate that is the internet needs to let off steam. It needs to have a bit of fun. So when it was asked what to name this new polar research ship, it of course went for something entirely practical. When offered names of great symbolism with the opportunity to lionize the great Antarctic explorers of old, the good people of the internet went in a different direction. They voted in overwhelming numbers for the name 'Boaty McBoatface'.

The popular will did not prevail in this case. The ship was instead christened the RRS *Sir David Attenborough*, in honour of the pioneering British broadcaster of nature programmes. The moral of the story is that names matter. There is dignity, identity and seriousness of purpose bound up in names. This applies as much to place names as it does to the marine world.

So what do you do if the name of your town no longer works for you? Do you stick with it or try to change things? History consistently suggests that it's the latter. We try and give messages through the names we find important. St Petersburg and Leningrad. Istanbul and Constantinople. New York and New Amsterdam. Names change when communities decide that names matter.

In Canada, there is a small town to the east of Montreal in the province of Quebec. It has a population of around 7,000 people. In the nineteenth century, it was named in honour of the source of its wealth – the resource it was synonymous with. The town's name was Asbestos. At the time it would have seemed like an unremarkable choice. But history has a way of making fools of us all, if we give it long enough.

For a while, asbestos had seemed a miracle product. Fire- and water-resistant, it was widely used in house construction and for insulation right across the world. No more. The evidence on asbestos has now been clear for some time. It has been shown to be a carcinogen that is deeply damaging to human lungs. Its effects kill people. Part of the devastation associated with its impact is that it operates as a ticking medical time bomb in people who have experienced high levels of asbestos exposure. It sits inside them for years and can appear decades later as an illness called mesothelioma, and is also a cause of lung cancer. In the UK, different types of asbestos were banned in 1985 and 1999. In Australia a total ban came into effect in 2003. In both countries, hundreds if not thousands of people continue to die each year from mesothelioma. It is a slow-burning legacy.

There is a town in outback Western Australia called Wittenoom. Actually, that's not quite right, because the town has been 'degazetted'. Officially, it no longer exists. For nearly three decades in the mid-twentieth century, Wittenoom was a booming mining town, producing blue asbestos. The site is now marked by a sign warning people not to go there. It sits at the heart of an area 120,000 acres in size that has been declared a contaminated site. Why? Because even now, over half a century since mining ceased, asbestos fibres and dust are present and 'may be airborne' (as the sign warns). That's how long-lasting the threat is, and how dangerous the substance is.

Many years of medical research have demonstrated that the highest rates of mesothelioma are associated, not surprisingly, with the people who worked most closely with it. The miners who dug it up, the handlers who carried and transported sacks of the material; the warehouse workers and the dockers who were part of the distribution chain. Stories abound about how these people would come home from work covered in dust, not realizing the danger this posed to them and to their families as clothes were shaken out and washed.

Like Australia, Canada was once a major producer and exporter of asbestos. It too had its mining towns and regions. That included the town of Asbestos in Quebec. Canada, in fact, continued to mine asbestos long after it had been abandoned in other places. It's a not-dissimilar dynamic to the one currently being faced by coal-mining towns around the world, as climate-change action pushes energy production further away from coal. Managed decline is an extraordinary political and policy challenge for governments. How do you tell people that you are depriving them of their livelihood – for the greater good? The greater good is a powerful force, but it doesn't put food on the table of miners who have just lost their jobs. The greater good provides little immediate comfort for those who lose the dignity of work.

So politicians are in a bind. They know without doubt when something has to change. You can't just keep mining asbestos, as if there's no medical link to mesothelioma, just to keep a town going. There is a public policy imperative to act. But leaders also know that it will – in the short term – lead to political pain. Very few voters line up to thank a government at the ballot box for stripping away their livelihoods. They're much more likely to vote for someone who tells them they've been hard done by, or who has tried hard to keep their local industries alive for longer.

Politicians find it hard to resist such electoral arithmetic. So they try to defend the status quo for as long as they can. What brings them down, in the end, is the data and evidence. It becomes too stark and too overwhelming to try and spin away. That's what happened to the asbestos industry in Canada. A decade ago, it was beyond clear that asbestos was a killer. The Canadian government knew it because, *within* Canada, asbestos was being removed from existing buildings due to the health dangers.

But in Quebec, the mines were still digging out asbestos. Hundreds if not thousands of local jobs depended either directly or indirectly on mining. In response, the government dug itself into a different kind of hole. Even as the product was being retroactively removed within Canada itself, the government was saying it could continue to be mined and exported as it was capable of being used safely. Canada worked hard internationally to successfully prevent asbestos being listed as a hazardous chemical under the appropriate international instruments. A critic might describe that as hypocrisy. A pragmatist might just say that's politics. Few would say it was a sustainable approach to policymaking.

But internationally, the relevant meeting that decides hazardous listings happens only once every two years, and decisions to list substances are by consensus. The relevant agreement is called the Rotterdam Convention, a UN agreement established in 1998 and in force since 2004. Canada was one of only a handful of signatories to the convention that refused in 2011 to support the listing of chrysotile asbestos as a hazardous chemical. It was continuing its established policy on the topic.

The majority of asbestos exports from Canada were to developing countries, where the mineral worked as an additive to products like cement, pipes, road surfaces and the like. The dangers are obvious. Critics had plenty to say in news reports and scientific journals. The president of the Canadian Medical Association, Jeff Turnbull, argued: 'We have a social responsibility to protect not only the health of Canadians but that of citizens elsewhere who are being harmed by a Canadian export. Canada should not be abdicating this responsibility.'[20] NDP politician Pat Martin put it more bluntly, suggesting that Canada was 'exporting human misery on a monumental scale'.[21] A 2008 report for the Rideau Institute, titled, 'Exporting Harm: How Canada Markets Asbestos to the Developing World', accused the Canadian government of giving funding to the asbestos lobby and promoting misinformation.[22]

The irony is that the Canadian government held the line just as the Canadian asbestos industry was caving in on itself anyway (although proposals for expansion remained on the table for a while). The Jeffrey Mine at Asbestos – once the biggest white asbestos mine on the planet – finally closed down in 2011–12. With it went the Canadian government's narrative that chrysotile asbestos was indeed a substance capable of being used safely. In 2012, the federal Industry minister, Christian Paradis, announced that the government would now support asbestos being listed as a hazardous substance under the Rotterdam Convention.

The case is another illustration that even the most determined government cannot outrun the evidence for ever. Political spin matters. Political determination to resist inconvenient truths is powerful and can slow things down for a while. That is how democracy is supposed to work. Finding good public policy decisions means listening to communities and responding to their concerns. But it also means facing the harsh realities of the data. When groups like the World Health Organization, the Canadian Medical Association, and the Canadian Cancer Society point to evidence that asbestos kills people, that evidence starts to have a cumulative effect. Canada had defied gravity longer than one might have expected, given the sheer number of countries banning the use of asbestos. Eventually, change had to come.

Which leads us back to the small town of Asbestos. Fans of the 1989 film *Dead Poets Society* will recall the scene where Robin Williams's character – the inspirational English teacher Mr Keating – urges one of his students with a downbeat surname to not let his name define him. It is a wonderful sentiment, but it doesn't work for everybody. Sometimes people decide that they'd rather change their name and forge a new identity altogether.

That was the conclusion reached by the citizens of Asbestos, Canada. The population of around 7,000 people settled the matter by voting for a new name in 2020. They chose 'Valdes-Sources' as the new name to take them forward into a new era. Press reports show that the town has been working hard since the mine's closure to diversify its appeal into new areas like food processing, ski tourism, and an award-winning brewery.[23] Time will tell whether the name change makes the desired difference.

What the town-formerly-known-as-Asbestos teaches us is that citizens understand when there is a disconnect between a story and the facts. The town itself may have a good story to tell. The town's name no longer does, so it needed to be changed. The people of the town know what it took the Canadian government itself too long to accept – that the evidence on the effects of asbestos simply doesn't align with a story that this is a safe product which should be exported to other parts of the world. Those ducks just aren't in a row. When that happens, something needs to give way. For this town, it was a name change. For governments, it's often a policy rethink that is required. They need to identify an action capable of meeting the exigencies of the moment whilst staying in alignment with the problem and the story they want to tell.

4. What Should We Do?

A prematurely aged man looks in the mirror. He's ostensibly in his prime, but already he wonders if life has passed him by. Is this really all there is? The job's OK, but unexciting. The family are great but getting on with their own stuff, and don't really pay him much heed. He can feel a strange clicking sound starting in his hip when he walks a certain way. There seem to be more grey hairs than dark when he goes to the hairdresser. He can't remember the last time he felt a surge of adrenalin about anything at all really. These introspective thoughts meld together and point towards one inevitable change that needs to be made. What is needed here is an expensive red sports car to restore life's balance and remind the world that he is an attractive, successful, still-young man.

The classic if somewhat mythical midlife crisis gives an insight into the slightly irrational ways in which humans often make decisions. There are actually studies now which argue that our mid-forties are indeed the most depressing time of life.[1] The balance of things to worry about is at its absolute worst. As we all know, there are of course many things that we can do to make our lives feel better. See a counsellor, take up a new hobby, try and exercise a little more and eat a little better; make some new friends. What demonstrably does not seem to work is buying a sports car. The intervention does not match the problem. The problem is multifaceted, and we tell ourselves all sorts of internal stories about it. We pick and choose the evidence from our lives that matches those stories. And then we buy a sports car.

Governments do the same thing. Just like our midlife-crisis man, they jump at the chance to take action and then look surprised when it doesn't fix the problem. Governments like to be seen to be 'doing' things. Once a problem has sprung into the public consciousness, political leaders can't run the risk of being seen to ignore it. Policy interventions are the actions that governments actually take in response to the problems they've identified. Issues arise when the proposed solution doesn't seem to match with the story being told about it or the facts underpinning it.

It is inherent in the nature of democracy that governments must be seen as responsive to their citizens. Whilst this responsiveness is undoubtedly one of the strengths of the democratic model, it also creates a dilemma for governments who are pushed to act when there might be many good reasons not to. They might end up applying what have been called 'Band-Aid' policies, which might signal that they are listening, but may not actually address the problem that needs fixing. At other times, governments may put in place measures they think will be popular, but without thinking through all the repercussions.

The results in the short term are often politically positive. Being *seen* to act helps to push an issue off the table. It ceases to be one of the immediate problems a government needs to grapple with. But the lack of alignment shows through, ultimately, in the form of diminishing trust in government. Critics are not assuaged by a policy intervention that self-evidently is not capable of actually addressing the issue. Instead of being extinguished, a problem continues to bubble away just below the surface, like a seemingly dormant volcano whose next eruption actually remains inevitable.

King George III has received something of a tough historical press in the United States. No one is printing *his* image onto a mug and getting sales. The problem might have begun before the Declaration of Independence, but was usefully summed up within its text: 'The history of the present King of Great Britain is a history of repeated injuries and usurpations, all having in direct object the establishment of an absolute Tyranny over these States'. The presence of such tyranny was sufficient to galvanize thirteen disparate colonies into armed struggle against their oppressor. It was an idea that was fused into the cultural fabric of the new nation that emerged.

From the very outset of the United States, the greatest threat of all was to fall under the tyranny of others. George III and his historical reputation were merely the personification of one of the strongest sentiments within American national life. As the state motto of New Hampshire so famously puts it, Americans must 'Live Free or Die'. The prevention of tyranny is not just a collective duty but also an individual imperative. People have the inalienable right to respond when tyranny threatens their liberty. To guarantee that people have the tools to protect themselves from the dangers of such tyranny, the founders created the Second Amendment to the

American Constitution, ratified in 1791. What it enshrined was the right to bear arms. Americans have been arguing about exactly what that means ever since.

There is no more emotive issue in American politics than what to do about guns. American rates of gun violence have been well documented for decades as by far the worst in the developed world. Each year, nearly 40,000 Americans die from gun violence. Both proponents and opponents of gun reform agree that there is a problem. There is little real dispute that the statistics are pretty accurate. So the data and evidence are there. But the opposing sides tell very different political stories about the nature and causes of gun violence. Those stories then lead to suggestions for policy fixes that offer little in the way of real change. Most suggested reforms to restrict the sale of guns fall far short of what comparative international evidence suggests would be needed. Similarly, those who suggest that the answer is to allow greater access to guns so that people can better defend themselves struggle to match that view with the realities of gun violence on the ground. So, whilst the data on gun violence are clear, the policy interventions are not.

There is a theory in public policy suggesting that problems which exist beneath the surface burst out on to the public agenda after key events have focused the minds of politicians on them.[2] The United States has proved time and again that the debate on what to do about gun violence springs most virulently into life in the aftermath of mass shootings. These are the moments when philosophical debates transform into shocking realities. Moments when politicians are asked some very hard questions on where they stand.

Amongst the many awful tragedies, the Sandy Hook school shooting stands out unusually starkly. A day of unspeakable heartbreak unfolded just before Christmas 2012 in Newtown, Connecticut, as a young man walked into an elementary school and gunned down twenty children in cold blood. Six staff members were also murdered, with the man's own mother having been the first victim earlier in the day.

The outpouring of grief was immediate and overwhelming. It radiated outwards from the bereaved parents, to the wider school community, the town, the state, and the country. President Obama walked to the podium in the White House Briefing Room to deliver heart-wrenching words to the nation as the events of the day became clear. He announced: 'This evening, Michelle and I will do what I know every parent in America will do, which is hug our children a little tighter, and we'll tell them that we love them, and we'll remind each other how deeply we love one another. But there are families in Connecticut who cannot do that tonight. And they need all of us right now. In the hard days to come, that community needs us to be at our best as Americans.'[3]

It was a moment of national devastation. A day of reckoning. A moment when the issue of what to do about gun violence once more moved from the edges of policymaking to the very heart of the American body politic.

But having arrived there, what quickly became clear is that agreement on what to actually do about the issue was no closer to emerging. Even in the face of such tragedy, stark ideological differences remained in the narratives told about gun violence, which then flowed through to the policy interventions recommended in response.

The pro-gun lobby traditionally focuses on individual responsibility. For them, the gun is simply the tool, it is perpetrators who are the problem. No organization captures that view more strongly than the National Rifle Association (NRA), for so long one of the most powerful issue lobby groups in America. As NRA head Wayne LaPierre put it after Sandy Hook: 'The truth is that our society is populated by an unknown number of genuine monsters – people so deranged, so evil, so possessed by voices and driven by demons that no sane person can possibly ever comprehend them.'[4] The way to beat such monsters was to make sure others were armed too. 'The only thing that stops a bad guy with a gun is a good guy with a gun.'

The politics on guns has long remained difficult, in part because the opinions of the American public have remained split. An opinion poll published a few months after the shooting attempted to capture whether the event had changed people's sentiments about guns. The poll found that it hadn't done so, at least not significantly. Research suggests that there has been relative stability for decades in how Americans view guns.[5] A large majority support background checks on gun purchasers, and smaller majorities support limits on the most dangerous military-type weaponry. But there is no majority support for banning guns. As researcher Kevin Wozniak has explained, the partisan lines in Congress on the issue reflect the equally strong partisan adherence in the wider community.[6] The result is policy gridlock.

The ducks are not just out of line, they are swimming in confused circles. Critics of gun reform start by pointing back to the kind of tyranny once associated with George III. 'The very purpose of the Second Amendment is to stop the government from disallowing people the means to defend themselves against tyranny', stated Congressman Steve Stockman in 2013. The issue, of course, is that some people are using their guns in ways that have nothing to do with protection against tyranny. So the question becomes: how can the government work to prevent citizens from shooting their fellow Americans without infringing on deeply held beliefs about the right to bear arms? That, in a very rough and tragic nutshell, is the essence of the problem for which politics has thus far been unable to produce a solution.

For some pro-gun advocates, the way to fix things is with more guns rather than less. There would be fewer school shootings, the logic goes, if teachers were armed and could immediately defend themselves and their students if they came under attack. It's a brutal logic which at first glance seems to offer the opportunity for alignment. It suggests that the 'problem' to be fixed is that unstable people go on shooting rampages. This aligns perfectly well with the data and evidence, which show that these rampages are in fact occurring with depressing regularity. That aligns with a political story about the right to bear arms and the long traditions associated with that idea. What swamps the alignment in the end is that the policy interventions that emerge from that logic are incredibly unlikely to achieve the desired results. Whilst comprehensive evidence on this policy idea remains limited, the research so far provides little cause for optimism.[7]

It is enormously difficult to change an entire national culture about guns just by nibbling around the edges of gun reform. Even in the wake of the most terrible tragedies, the reforms proposed to date have not been particularly dramatic. They have tended to focus on improving background checks, and closing loopholes associated with sales direct to customers at gun shows. The stark reality is that even these small changes, which have been politically so contentious, are actually likely to achieve little in preventing gun crime. The shooter at Sandy Hook used a gun that had been purchased and was owned legally by his mother.

Evidence from overseas suggests that much more dramatic action is needed if the goal is to decrease the number of guns out in the community. That is the lesson from Australia, amongst other places. When a lone gunman unleashed terror in April 1996 at Port Arthur in Tasmania, the human toll was catastrophic, with thirty-five dead and twenty-three injured. The event carved a scar into the Australian psyche in relation to gun crimes. Newly elected Prime Minister John Howard, from the conservative side of Australian politics, oversaw the introduction of some of the toughest gun laws in the world immediately after that event. This was supported by a mandatory gun buy-back scheme, under which the government spent AUD\$350 million on buying and destroying well over half a million guns. The number of gun deaths in Australia per annum has reduced significantly since, for complex and multiple reasons.[8] Overall, the evidence is clear that extensive gun-law reform correlates with fewer gun deaths.[9]

The central question comes back to the definition of the problem. The low-tolerance approach of the Australian laws sees guns themselves as part of the problem. Certain high-powered, semi-automatic weapons are seen as having no place in domestic homes. That is then coupled with a careful licence and regulation regime to make sure that all gun sales are recorded, so that it is always clear who has a gun and how it was obtained.

The dominant problem definition in the USA is that people are the problem, not guns. Under this kind of definition, there's no point trying to outlaw certain gun sales because guns aren't the problem. You can't legislate against 'evil', so you can't do anything about 'evil' people choosing to shoot others with guns. If you can't really tell who is 'angry' enough to want to shoot someone else, you can't do much to prevent it. All that is left is to concentrate on supporting the wider availability of guns so that people can defend themselves in the event of an attack.

The depth of the divide was evident soon after Sandy Hook. The tragedy initially acted as a spur to action. The Obama administration almost immediately advocated for legislative change. The president signed a slew of new executive orders to tackle gun violence, and Vice-President Joe Biden was placed at the head of a gun violence taskforce.

But of course, presidents cannot create legislative change by themselves in the US system. That task falls to Congress, so it was here that the debate got tough. A proposal for an Assault Weapons Ban was defeated 60–40 in the Senate. A proposal in favour of tightening background checks, known as the Manchin-Toomey amendment after its main sponsors, also went down to defeat. At the same time, there was a spike in gun sales out in the community, presumably as people sought to get in ahead of any changes to legislation that might tighten restrictions on gun ownership. The gun divide was on display for all to see.

At the time of writing, nearly ten years on from Sandy

Hook, another wave of tragedy has just been unleashed. On 24 May 2022, a lone attacker shot dead nineteen children and two teachers at a school in Uvalde, Texas. After the initial shock, the same two narratives about guns and gun-crime emerged once more. But this time, the first glimmer of agreement has also been forged. The searing physical and emotional cost of another school mass shooting underpinned a rare congressional agreement to reach for change. *The Bipartisan Safer Communities Act*, passed in June 2022, strengthens criminal background checks, funds mental health support, and restricts gun ownership by domestic violence perpetrators. It remains to be seen whether these new laws can match the scale of the policy challenge at hand.

A misalignment between problems and solutions is – thankfully – not always as entrenched as it is for something like gun reform. However, the same issue can emerge in the most unexpected places, when governments don't stop to think through the potential unintended consequences of their choices. They sometimes don't look enough before they jump. As a result, they can land in the wrong place, as the Danish government found out to its cost in 2011.

It's a bracing business, leaping suddenly into ice-cold water. It's meant to shock, both physically and mentally. It takes a particular mindset to seek out such a shock. Especially in winter, most of us prefer to cosy up somewhere away from the elements. This is often accompanied by the eating of comfort food, parked in front of the heater, waiting for the spring sunshine to reawaken us into action. Why push ourselves deliberately into discomfort?

One answer is that exercise is widely accepted as providing extraordinary health benefits. It seems an easy way to combat two of the most common issues confronting the Western world – an obesity crisis and a mental-health crisis. In Denmark, as in so much of Scandinavia, the pursuit of well-being has become something of a cultural trademark, long predating the contemporary embrace of the idea. Just look at the folk at the Det Kolde Gys swimming club in Copenhagen. This hardy group, founded in 1929, meet at the Helgoland sea baths for winter swimming in water that is literally ice-cold. You can tell it's that cold because apparently there is often ice floating around in it. But it would be hard to know for sure, because some members like to swim early, before the sunrise, so not only are they swimming with ice, but they are doing so in the dark. You'd have to be crazy, right? Well, maybe. But there are a reported eighty-plus cold-water swimming clubs in Denmark. Det Kolde Gys alone has 2,000 members – and apparently a waiting list.[10]

The Danes understand what good health means. According to the Eurobarometer on sport and physical activity – published by the European Commission in 2018 – only 20 per cent of Danes say that they never exercise or play sport. How does that compare to the rest of Europe? Well, only two countries do better. No prizes for guessing that they are Finland and Sweden.[11] The benefits are clear. According to Statista, in 2016 Denmark had the lowest obesity rates in the EU – at 19.7 per cent. By comparison, the UK had the second highest rate with 27.8 per cent categorized as obese.[12]

Denmark looks like a pretty good place to be. By world standards, life is good. Its people are healthy and happy on most comparative measures. As far as obesity goes, the Danish seem to have less to worry about than many other developed nations. But if that's the case, why did the Danish government introduce a 'fat tax' in 2011, adding a levy to all products based on the level of saturated fat they contain? History shows that it was to be a short-lived policy experiment. It only took a year for the measure to be withdrawn, as an array of unintended economic and social consequences emerged. Looking back, it was a policy solution that proved unable to align with both the evidence and the narrative on why it was necessary.

When it was introduced in 2011, this Danish tax was the first of its kind in the world. It was specifically targeted at increasing the price of foods with high fat contents. As a result, things like meat and dairy products saw prices rise. The fact that Denmark was and remains a large exporter of exactly these type of products to the rest of the world was not lost on contemporary commentators, who detected an irony in the arrangement.[13] Many researchers are also not convinced that obesity is best tackled by a 'fat tax' of this kind.[14] Sugar and salt are seen as much better targets if the government is looking to the tax system to nudge people towards better health.

So just what did the Danish government think it was doing in unleashing something that would prove to be quite so dramatically unpopular? Numerous studies and reviews have started to look back at the story of the Danish fat tax to pick apart what went wrong. The policy seemed to start for all the 'right' reasons. The problem definition was certainly based on a public health rationale, at least at the proposal stage. Even then, though, it was clear that the potential health effects were not necessarily game-changing in themselves. A report by the Disease Prevention Commission in 2009 projected that a fat tax would lead to an increase in average life expectancy of only five days, based on an expected tiny reduction in heart disease.[15] Still, the government was careful to have a full consultation process, with a focus on groups in the food industry in particular, as they sought to understand the potential economic impacts of the tax. There was little opposition in Parliament to the introduction of the measure. In Denmark's multi-party proportional Parliament, only a handful of members voted to oppose the new tax.

It all seemed to go so smoothly. Here was a measure, based on extensive consultation and assessment, which passed with overwhelming cross-party support in the Danish Parliament, including from parties not a part of the government. This looks like clear policy success. Sure, there were some criticisms and warnings from parts of industry, but little hint of the furore that was to come.

The tax began to unravel when it became clear that its impact as a policy intervention just didn't fit with a clear story of why it was necessary and what it was hoping to achieve. The narrative about the public health benefits was undermined by experts, who argued it was actually a poorly designed and targeted tax. There was also little consensus that saturated fats were sufficiently dangerous to warrant this approach. This was accompanied by a slew of complaints from industry groups. As consumers started to take their business elsewhere, and elements of the food industry struggled with the increased administrative regulation, the tax soon found itself politically friendless.

The real irony is that we do not really know – based on the Danish experiment – whether the 'fat tax' was having a beneficial overall public health impact. After getting dumped only a year into its life, the data can't tell us much. There are hints that it was providing at least some benefit. Studies have suggested that Danes did actually consume less fat whilst it was in operation.[16] It also raised US$216 million in government revenue. But, in a way, such positives didn't matter. The politics went wrong because the intervention didn't align. The problem wasn't actually compelling enough, meaning the narrative didn't take root effectively enough, and the evidence suggested Denmark was already one of the healthiest places in Europe in any case.

What's more, the decision to axe the tax after only a year highlighted that the economic imperatives far outweighed the public health ones in the government's mind. The government was not prepared to hold on to a tax which promised hardly any benefits in long-term public health in return for considerable short-term political aggravation. The media were also highlighting stories which collectively did little to increase public confidence in the tax. There were allegations of businesses hiking prices higher than justified and using the tax as an excuse. There were suggestions that lower-income families were being the hardest hit by the price rise, exacerbating existing social inequalities. And finally, there were job losses in the food industry at a time when the Danish economy was still struggling to recover from the 2008 financial crisis.[17] The collective weight of those criticisms became too much to bear.

Whilst it was introduced on public health grounds, what caused the tax to flounder had very little to do with people's physical well-being. It was the economic hit that hurt. Evidence suggests that consumers were starting to cross the border to Germany to buy things that they'd always seen as staples. What started as a recipe for healthier bodies finished as a formula for angry voters. As summed up by the then minister for Food, Agriculture and Fisheries, Mette Gjerskov, 'the fat tax is one of the most maligned we had in a long time'.[18]

There were many reasons that the ducks wouldn't get in a row. The problem was poorly defined. The narrative was weakly put together. Vague promises to boost people's health were not enough to help underpin the policy once the criticisms really got going. The data and evidence, even from the public health professionals, did not suggest that dramatic health improvements would flow from the measure. Finally, the tax itself, when it came, was poorly designed and targeted, causing immediate resentment from businesses and consumers alike. It was the wrong policy intervention. What had looked like a policy walk in the park ended up as a policy lead balloon. A measure that had passed Parliament with the overwhelming support of elected representatives was repealed just a year later by a similarly overwhelming majority. Quite a turnaround. The government got the politics of policymaking wrong, and they paid the price.

Just imagine the gentle bobbing of the waves beneath your surfboard. The water's warm . . . because it always is in Australia. The sun's shining . . . because it always is in Australia. As you straddle a piece of fibreglass and wait for the next wave, you take a moment to contemplate life and how good it is. You're only fifty metres or so away from golden sands.

You've still got a few grains of that sand stuck to your hair, baked on by a mixture of salt water and sunshine. For you, it's just a normal day. While others around the country and around the world are striving to create wealth, you've decided to soak up nature's riches instead. The guy running the shop where you bought your morning coffee asks you whether you've got a job to go to. Standing there in your half-undone wetsuit, you just shake your head and smile.

'Nah mate. Can't be f**ked.'

This mythical figure is ingrained in the Australian psyche. There are confirmed sightings each year. This iconic figment of the national imagination is none other than the Australian 'dole bludger'. The genus is known as a lazy good-for-nothing who would rather live off the work of the taxpayers paying the welfare cheques than actually go out and get a job. The dole bludger is like the monsters under your childhood bed. Always lurking, ready to steal from the government's coffers, but remarkably hard to find when you actually turn on the light to go and investigate.

The dole bludger is, of course, an invention. He is an idea (I say 'he' because the original conception was overwhelmingly of a male), brought to life by the political rhetoric of governments in the 1970s, trying to somehow divest themselves of blame for high unemployment rates. Instead of the unemployed being the victims of wider economic forces, in the 1970s they were recast as being the victims of their own lack of ambition. There were plenty of jobs available, if only people were willing to work hard and not be so picky. After the social generosity of the post-war decades, the 1970s resurrected the social tropes that had underpinned Victorian ideas of the difference between the deserving and the undeserving poor.

The dole bludger represented not just an economic danger but also a moral one. People who are willing to sink so low as to allow someone else to support them must undoubtedly also suffer from other moral failings. Not content with laziness, they are surely also people who will take what they can get when they can get it. In other words, they'll steal what they're not entitled to. You have to watch them like a hawk when handing out government money.

That, at least, was the underlying narrative apparent in the Australian government's attitude towards welfare claimants in 2015. There was a belief within government that the welfare system was essentially being ripped off. People were believed to be claiming social security benefits that they were not entitled to. There was undoubtedly an ideological element behind those beliefs, but it is of course also true that governments do have a responsibility to ensure that taxpayers' money is being spent wisely. So, if you are in government and you believe some citizens are ripping off the system, how can you find out for sure?

One way is to audit the accounts and circumstances of every individual receiving some kind of welfare payment. The immediate problem you face is one of scale. We're talking millions of people who would need to be investigated. The person-hours required to individually audit the complete financial records of everyone who has received a welfare payment would be eye-watering. The resources required would likely far outweigh any economic benefit from repayments, even if fraud was in fact discovered.

But if humans can't do it, maybe a machine can? They're pretty smart now, machines. Algorithms and artificial intelligence have got policymakers worldwide excited for all sorts of reasons. The promise is undeniably exciting. But the problem remains that machines still lack a certain discernment. As good as the technology is, it still struggles with discretion and nuanced judgements. If you set it to work with instructions that aren't sufficiently well thought-through, the result might not be as expected.

That is exactly what happened to the Australian government when it decided to use computers to seek out welfare fraud. In what has become known as the 'robodebt' scandal, in 2015 the government announced its intention to recover many hundreds of millions of dollars worth of 'overpayments' that had been claimed on social security benefits. From 2016, for several years, it swung that programme into action by putting its computers to work. In essence, the policy implementation relied on a form of data-matching. Computers ran the social security records of individuals against their tax return records. If the programme suggested someone had claimed something they were not entitled to, they were issued with a demand for the money. People who had been happily going about their lives thinking they had their finances under control were suddenly hit with a debt demand that – until that moment – had not even existed.

As it turned out, there were several problems with this approach. Firstly, the courts found the programme to be unlawful. Secondly, many of the alleged mismatches between records were incorrectly identified as overpayments. And thirdly, the government pushed on, even when it was made aware of concerns about the potential illegality and evidence of mismatching.

The process was enormously costly in terms of the stress experienced by thousands of Australians who were chased for debts that weren't real. There are allegations that the scheme contributed to some people taking their own lives. In all, more than 350,000 people found themselves directly pursued for payment by their own government. But it was costly financially too, because those 350,000-plus people pursued a class action lawsuit once the true extent of the policy mistake became apparent. The government settled the case for a total of $1.2 billion, agreeing to repay over $700 million in 'overpayments' that had been clawed back, drop further claims worth hundreds of millions, and pay a total of over $110 million compensation to the individuals who had been incorrectly targeted.[19] Multiple reports by oversight bodies like the Ombudsman and Senate committees, not to mention court action, confirmed at multiple stages what the final court settlement made obvious: that this was a policy debacle of staggering proportions.

In truth, this went wrong at most stops along the way. The problem definition – the alleged defrauding of the welfare system – was dramatically overstated. Nevertheless, having 'found' the problem, the government pushed on with a narrative that aligned with it. Taxpayers' money should not be wasted, so people who had nothing to hide should equally have nothing to fear from having their records checked. When he was minister for Social Security, Scott Morrison said in a TV interview that Australians wouldn't put up with people ripping off the system, and that there needed to be a 'strong welfare cop on the beat'.[20] His successor in the job, Christian

Porter, emphasized that 'this is not a matter of apology . . . there are a massive amount of overpayments that occur in the system, now we are actually tackling that problem.'[21]

The data and evidence were undoubtedly expected to bear this out when the data-matching began. And there is no denying that some overpayments do occur. There are debts that are legitimately owed to the government coffers (although many result from human error rather than malicious fraud). It is perhaps unsurprising that the government was confident that there was money to be found. The measure was initially projected to save $1.7 billion in five years. Those projections increased to more than $3 billion as the programme continued. As former US Senator Everett McKinley was once misquoted as saying: 'a billion here, a billion there; pretty soon you're talking about real money'.

It sounds too good to be true. And indeed it was. The government simply didn't get its ducks in a row. If there really was financial misappropriation on the scale anticipated, then a simple piece of data-matching was never going to be sophisticated enough to reveal it. Tax is complex. Ever wonder why so many people employ a taxation agent to do their tax return? And social security payments are also anything but a simple 'one-size-fits-all' calculation. The timing of wages payments, the changing amounts and variation in circumstances require closer scrutiny than a data-matching programme could provide. Individual case handlers were needed to apply human judgement. That's how the system had worked up until that point, and the robodebt fiasco revealed why.

There has been a wide embrace by policymakers around the world in the last decade of something called 'nudge' policy.

The idea, grounded in insights from behavioural economics, is that citizens can be 'nudged' towards preferred outcomes by the decision-making architecture that is placed around their choices. The classic example is something like organ donation. If people are required to actively tick a box to say that they'd be happy to donate their organs in case of a fatal accident, many don't bother to do so. But if you reverse the architecture by asking them to tick the box to *opt out* of organ donation, most still won't bother to tick the box. It's a quick decision-making moment that can actually save lives. Setting that choice up in a way that nudges people towards generosity has been extraordinarily successful in multiple countries.

The robodebt scheme reflects a similar kind of nudge architecture at its core. If you just ask citizens to look at their own records and identify any overpayments and pay them back, you aren't going to get very far. So instead, you generate a letter telling them that they have a debt and put the onus on them to disprove it. It jolts them into action. It's nudging . . . but of the kind more familiar to a nightclub bouncer than government departments. It's nudging with a fiscal baseball bat, in support of a policy goal that was far too complex for the approach adopted. The government chose the wrong intervention and paid the price for that mistake.

All governments find themselves in this position on occasion. The result is that the policy ducks stay stubbornly out of alignment and perceptions of policy success slip away. No wonder politicians often look stressed. The good news is that – even in the face of complexity and difficulty – better outcomes are possible, as the next chapter illustrates.

5. Ducks in a Row:
What Success Looks Like

It is so seductive, isn't it? The gentle curl of the smoke from a cigarette. The smell of the tobacco. The look of sophistication embodied in Don Draper's nonchalant holding of a cigarette in one hand, with a glass in the other. When I was growing up in Australia in the 1980s, smoking seemed simultaneously rebellious and grown-up. Marlboro Man ads were in every corner shop. The height of disdain for authority was to ride your BMX bike to one of those shops and convince the owners in that less cautious age that they should sell you a packet of smokes. Unfortunately, due to the curse of a good upbringing, I couldn't bring myself to join in the rebellion. I stayed outside to mind the bikes.

If you look at the statistics, smoking rates were actually already in decline during the 1980s, especially amongst Australian men. In the early 1960s, 58 per cent of men were smokers, double the rates amongst women. By the mid-1980s, this had come down to 33 per cent of men (whilst rates for women held remarkably steady in the high 20s).[1] But that still means that somewhere close to a third of Australian adults were addicted to tobacco. And the smoke was everywhere.

I was lucky enough to go on an international flight to Europe as a teenager in 1987 and the plane had a smoking section. It wasn't hidden behind some kind of all-encompassing plastic screen. As many readers will remember, the smoking seats just started behind rows that were non-smoking. There was little real demarcation. No fancy smoke extractors to make the smoke disappear. In order to trek back to the toilets, you had to wave your way through clouds that just hung in the air.

Fast-forward to 2019 and the number of Australian adults who smoke is down to 11.6 per cent.[2] Not only can you no longer smoke on the plane, you can't even smoke in the terminal building. In fact, you can't smoke within four metres of the entrance to such a building. You can't smoke in pubs or clubs. Smokers across the country find themselves huddled instead in small outside corners that have been set aside solely for the purpose of dragging in a quick nicotine hit. There's no Don Draper moment here. No languid reclining whilst 'enjoying' a cigarette. Things have changed.

The health benefits are obvious. Coronary heart disease, lung cancer, and strokes are all big killers in Australia, and smoking increases your chances of getting any or all of them. Mind you, we've known for decades that smoking isn't exactly good for you. We knew it even when my mates were riding those BMX bikes down to the corner shop to buy yet more cigarettes. The danger of the substance made its consumption cooler.

Not any more. The Australian Institute of Health and Welfare has undertaken the National Drug Strategy Household Survey every few years since 1985. One of the things it measures is levels of public opinion about the ever-increasing laws and rules around smoking. The results are extraordinary really. Support for the laws has stayed remarkably strong. That includes amongst smokers themselves. The 2019 survey confirms that support for increasing taxes on tobacco in order to pay for treatment and/or health education remains over 65 per cent. Australians have essentially been saying to their government for decades: keep making smoking harder, keep charging us more, and we'll keep loving you for it.

What the hell is going on here? There are of course many complicated, interconnected reasons for that result. Changes in public health awareness over time, the availability of other drugs, improvements in medical care and scientific understanding and so on. But there is also no doubt that successive governments have got their ducks in a row on this one. The problem crystallized not simply when data began to emerge that smoking was bad for you, but when data further showed that it was bad for those *around* you. That's the moment when a matter of making poor personal choices turned into something with wider moral implications. Civil libertarians might argue that they have the right to smoke themselves to death if they want to. It is a perfectly defensible argument at a certain level of abstraction. What is much less defensible is that the personal choices of one individual should increase someone else's chances of getting lung cancer.

Having decided that the problem is about protecting others from the choices of those who smoke, what exactly should a government do? The Prohibition era in the United States is a resonant warning from history that simply banning something entirely creates as many problems as it solves. It encourages black markets, leads to civil disobedience and angers people who want to enjoy the occasional drink without government interference. It's a lesson that has not been lost on Australian policymakers. Instead of banning smoking, they set out to make it undesirable and expensive. They focused the strongest legal measures not on blocking the sale of cigarettes to adults, but in restricting the right to smoke them around other people.

That's why Australians are not allowed to smoke when there are children in the car. They are also not allowed to smoke in or around school playgrounds. They can't light up in a restaurant, or on a train, or even inside the train station. The underlying message is really clear and consistent: smoke if you want to, but don't take anyone else down with you. Only 2.1 per cent of children now live in households where they are regularly exposed to someone else's cigarette smoke. That's down from nearly 20 per cent in 2001. If that's not a public policy triumph, I don't know what is.

The problem definition – duck number one – clicked firmly into place by focusing not only on the smoker but on those around the smoker. The data and evidence about the dangers of smoking has kept emerging ever since the links between smoking and serious disease were first discovered. That evidence has now been around for decades. It makes the job easier for governments because they don't have to 'prove' that smoking is a problem. There are no competing problem definitions fighting for attention. There has been little cut-through by any data and evidence suggesting that smoking brings any kind of health benefits. Unlike climate change, there are very few 'smoking deniers' out there who say smoking is a perfectly healthy activity. The arguments are around whether you should be free to do it anyway, not about whether it actually is as bad as the weight of evidence suggests.

In essence, the problem is clear, and the data and evidence back it up to the hilt. So far so good. As always, the biggest challenge is then to get the story right. Just what should the narrative be on this? Too much heavy-handed sermonizing from politicians may not be the best approach. Sitting in judgement on people struggling with nicotine addiction and telling them just to 'get their act together' might sound like scolding. People seldom take kindly to being told off by their government for anything.

Successive governments have been alert to the need to strike the right tone. Unlike stories about dole bludgers or people smugglers, smokers have not been categorized as the 'bad guys' of this narrative. A succession of smart policymakers haven't sought to bring down a deluge of moral judgement on the heads of people desperately lighting up on street corners. Instead, smokers are presented as the victims of this story. It's a story of redemption, as smokers turn their lives around in the face of an evil invention that has trapped them in their own addiction. People who quit are liberating themselves from the heavy hand of a noxious substance. Those who cannot yet escape the clutches of their addiction can at least save those that they love from its worst excesses. Choosing not to smoke around families and friends is an act of sacrifice you can make for those you love. Smokers have the chance to be a hero, without having to put up with being demonized first. It is a narrative that has proved remarkably successful over several decades.

Just as importantly, the first three ducks have swum through in full alignment with the policy interventions actually put in place. People don't get fined or thrown in jail for simply having a cigarette (as long as they're smoking in the right places). Instead, they get given support and encouragement to quit. This has come through government advertising, which encourages people to consider a healthier lifestyle. It has come through a financial hit as taxes on cigarettes continue to go up. In 2016 the government announced legislated increases in excise on cigarettes of 12.5 per cent every year for four years, with the stated goal of raising the price of a packet of cigarettes to AUD$40. Both major parties supported it. So did an overwhelming majority of voters. The price of cigarettes has increased by over 340 per cent since 1996,[3] and people are broadly happy about it! Not too many areas of public policy could say the same. But this has, of course, not been without some negative impacts too. Lower income smokers, addicted to nicotine and struggling to quit, have seen the percentage of their income going on their smoking habit skyrocket in recent years.

Perhaps the best-known intervention of the past two decades was the move to enforce the plain packaging of cigarettes. Australia was the first country to do so when it brought in the change in 2012. In the face of condemnation and legal action from tobacco companies, Australian governments have held firm. It's not hard to see why. Plain packaging breaks the link to the seductive images of the cigarette I referred to earlier. Looking at the Marlboro Man made you want to take up smoking. Other cigarette brands in Australia had wonderful yachts sailing on clear blue waters. The golden glow of a packet of Benson & Hedges on the shelves behind the store counter was powerful. And this was for a kid who didn't even smoke!

At a stroke, the Australian government took all that away. Where once you would have seen an image to make you dream, you can now see a diseased eyeball, held open by a kind of medical fish hook. The writing tells you that smoking causes blindness. And we're not talking in the small print – it is literally emblazoned across the pack. The goal is not just to encourage existing smokers to quit, but – even more importantly – to stop impressionistic young people from starting.

That is what success looks like. Well-targeted policies which are not unduly punitive, matched with a narrative that empowers rather than judges. None of that would matter if the data and evidence didn't also add up. Decades of health studies about smoking have laid that groundwork. Governments have simply needed to slot it into place in their policy thinking.

Australia's success in decreasing smoking rates is a notable policy achievement. But it is also a cautionary illustration of the restless nature of policy change. It didn't happen overnight and the fact that successive governments had their ducks in a row did not mean that there was no significant opposition. Far from it. There were high-profile legal challenges from tobacco companies that were not prepared just to accept defeat. And while support for the policy remains extraordinarily high, it has started to slip slightly in the last few years. Another policy problem in the making, perhaps. So political success is never absolute. It is conditional on the moment, and policies continue to evolve as more information rolls in. The ducks don't sit still.

*

You don't have to look far for strong opinions about Margaret Thatcher. When she died in April 2013, some voters danced in the street whilst expressing their disdain for the tenor of her rule.[4] Some writers and commentators, reflecting back on an influential life, thought that her complicated legacy had a dark undertone. A posthumous piece in *The Guardian* by one of Thatcher's biographers, Hugo Young, lamented Thatcher's role in shepherding in a Britain with a diminished sense of community. 'Whether pushing each other off the road, barging past social rivals, beating up rival soccer fans, or idolizing wealth as the only measure of virtue, Brits became more unpleasant to be with.'[5]

Other commentators took a very different view, lauding Thatcher for her policy achievements and for crashing through the glass ceiling as Britain's first woman prime minister. One of her successors as Conservative Party leader, Iain Duncan Smith, remembered her 'strength of character and her determination to lead no matter what the odds'.[6] Civil servants who had worked closely with her penned an op-ed which remembered her as 'a kind and considerate boss', who 'provided clear and consistent direction'.[7] Such was the tension of the moment that some Labour MPs, who recalled Thatcher with rather less equanimity, turned on those same civil servants for daring to make such positive comments. One suggested to the two civil service authors that they had 'prostituted your high office and deserted your political neutrality'.[8] A divisive figure in life remained a divisive figure in death.

A public opinion poll undertaken the day after Thatcher's death sought to gather people's views on her tenure and to identify some of her signature achievements. It was a mixed bag of results. Some policies were remembered fondly, whereas others remained reviled even thirty years later. But one policy in particular stood out as an iconic popular initiative, a rolled-gold political winner. This was the move to allow housing tenants to buy their council house. A full 65 per cent of Britons polled in 2013 looked back favourably on this as one of Thatcher's most transformational moves.[9] In many ways it is the policy that is most classically Thatcher. It's about small government rather than big government. It's about individual empowerment rather than community empowerment. And it's about building individual wealth rather than communal assets.

Thatcher herself saw it in that light. She highlighted the achievements of the programme in a 1984 speech to the National Housebuilding Council, extolling the virtues of home ownership.

'Since we took office in 1979, 1.7 million more people have come to own their homes – 1.7 million more sole kings upon their own sole ground . . . The greatest single contribution has come from giving council and public sector tenants the right to buy. Most council tenants, especially the younger ones, long for the chance to own their own homes. Indeed, home ownership is so popular that even the Opposition are coming round to it.'[10]

The last point was a poignant one. The opposition Labour Party had indeed initially opposed the policy (despite themselves having considered the idea some years before in an earlier manifesto). Such was its popularity that Labour had to change tack. There are few surer signs of a dominant political narrative than the fact that your own worst enemies have no choice but to support it. Right-to-buy commanded the field. The government had its ducks in a row.

To understand why it was so popular, we have to start by looking at what problem this idea was supposed to solve. All exercises in problem definition have political underpinnings built into them. That is especially so with something like housing. If you were a public policy specialist looking at housing, you might argue that the number one problem is to make sure everybody has a roof over their head. It doesn't matter who the roof actually belongs to, as long as everyone has safe and warm shelter. Success would equate to everyone having a home to live in. As appealing as that basic framing of the problem is, it ignores some key emotional, psychological and financial aspects that underpinned the political success of the right-to-buy initiative.

Research suggests that people draw deep psychological benefits from buying their own home. It feeds into long-standing ideas of what the 'home' is. The home is a sanctuary from the outside world. Phrases like 'every Englishman's home is his castle' have a connection into the national psyche, no matter how mythical in reality. The underlying sense is that your own home is where the dominion of the 'State' stops. This is a place where you can do what you want, when you want, without needing anyone's permission. It is only if you actually own the bricks and mortar that you can guarantee that sentiment. By definition, a council house is owned by someone else – some arm of the State – who is just 'letting' you live in it. At least that's one way of framing it, and it's the view that underpinned the success of the government's narrative on the change.

There are also undeniable financial benefits that come from owning your own home. Average house prices for existing dwellings in the UK have increased dramatically in recent decades.[11] If you have a foot on the housing ladder, those price rises seem like good news. The value of your home is going up, as is your overall wealth. It offers feelings of certainty and security. So there are strong reasons – financial, emotional and psychological – at play, into which the right-to-buy policy was able to tap. When looked at through that lens, the policy problem emerges reasonably clearly. The starting point is that home ownership is 'good' for people. Low-income families in council housing were struggling to access this 'good' thing by getting on the housing ladder in the conventional way.

It is not a hard story to sell to the electorate. The 1979 Tory manifesto framed home ownership as an aspirational goal, promising to place it at the heart of their vision for a 'property-owning democracy'. The Secretary of State for the Environment, Michael Heseltine, when speaking in the Commons shortly after the Conservative victory in 1979, described the government's measures on housing as 'no less than a framework for a social revolution'. He declared that: 'Too many of our people are forced to accept the restrictions of tenancy. We are determined to give them the freedom and opportunities of freeholders.'[12]

It's a rousing story. Tenants, instead of being seen as beneficiaries of the State's determination to provide them with housing, are characterized as being trapped by it, locked out of the financial and personal gains of home ownership. The government would release them from this state of incarceration that was holding them back. As a narrative, it has the benefit of not blaming tenants for their predicament. The villains of the piece – as Heseltine expounded it – were previous Labour policies and a bureaucracy intent on keeping down the entrepreneurial spirit of existing tenants.

It's a story that bears a similarity to the Australian cigarette narrative. The people each policy is targeting are not attacked as being at fault for their own predicament. The government is offering to help them fight their way out. It's government on a white steed, riding to the rescue, in order to allow people to be the best that they can be.

If one starts from the proposition that home ownership is a financial and moral good, there is also no shortage of data and evidence to back up that narrative. House prices had gone up enormously in the thirty years prior to 1979. And they have skyrocketed further in the forty years since. The research also supports the proposition that people who own their own home are likely to be happier, healthier, and even to see better education outcomes for their children.[13]

So, on the problem, the story being told about it, and the factual support available, things were in strong alignment. The ducks were ready to go. The intervention itself joined the conga line easily because it was designed in ways that reflect the other three aspects. The genius at the heart of right-to-buy was the discount rate offered to tenants who took it up. Not only could you have a legal right to buy the house you were occupying, but you could do so at up to half the normal market value. It offered a cut-price route to home ownership. That is the secret heart of the arrangement. If the problem is that home ownership is being denied, and the narrative is of people being trapped into tenancy, then the solution has to be more than *permission* to buy, it has to come with the *discount* that actually makes it possible.

The right-to-buy scheme was an undoubted and undeniable political success. But as with other examples in this book, political success is not necessarily synonymous with something being a 'good' longer-term policy idea.[14] There are many negatives that have flowed alongside the success of the right-to-buy scheme.[15] The narrative of individual opportunity that Thatcher's government intentionally pursued has come at a cost to community assets. The UK today has less public housing available than it did in 1979. Despite the fact that millions of people have successfully bought their council house, there remain millions who could not do so, and others who are now languishing on long waiting lists for the diminished public housing stock that is available.

Longer-term rates of inequality have also continued to widen, and the fate of those 'left behind' in the UK dominates the wider policy conversation today. So whatever else it was, right-to-buy was no magic bullet for solving poverty or homelessness. Nor was it any kind of sure-fire pathway to financial empowerment. All of those things are problematic and are sowing the seeds of future policy problems that will require solving in their turn. But none of these factors negate the political success of the policy at the time and since. The enduring depth of that success is reflected in the fact that the term 'right-to-buy' routinely reappears in conversations around election time as the Conservative Party pulls together its manifesto. The desire for new policies to be associated with this previous success is irresistible for politicians looking for a head start in the policy race.

*

For those of us who are fortunate enough to live in reasonably safe places, there are some things that we tend to take for granted. One is our physical safety when out in public. Despite the well-documented individual cases of violent crime on our streets, many of us are lucky enough to simply assume that we can come and go safely. What is more, we feel even safer in our own homes. With running water on tap, bathroom facilities, and cooking appliances, we are able to relax whilst attending to basic needs.

For too long, for millions of women and girls in India, that was not the case. For them an act as 'simple' as going to the toilet has been accompanied by a sense of danger, fear, even terror. That is because, until very recently, many Indian homes did not have access to sufficient sanitation facilities. That lack of access to 'private' toilet spaces left literally millions of women having to defecate in the open, in fields, with the constant danger of being watched or attacked. This is not some theoretical danger. There have been multiple well-documented and horrifying cases of rape and murder, alongside the countless 'everyday' crimes of abuse, intimidation and assault that women in India have had to confront as a result.[16]

Good sanitation doesn't sound like a particularly revolutionary public policy goal for those of us already fortunate enough to have it. But if you are unfortunate enough to be without it, the results can be absolutely devastating. Good sanitation saves lives in so many ways. For one thing, it prevents the spread of deadly diseases and infections. Diarrhoea, cholera and other devastating illnesses flourish in places where sanitation is poor. But in India the problem goes so much further, through other, less immediately noticeable impacts.

For instance, girls have been more likely to leave school early than boys because of the embarrassment and safety issues associated with not having access to safe, private toilet facilities. Through issues like these, open defecation emerges as a complex web of problems that goes far beyond questions of hygiene. The scale of what might be required to address such an issue is mind-boggling.

The core of the problem that India faced in dealing with open defecation is twofold. The first part of the problem might be seen as an infrastructure issue, in the well-documented fact that there have simply not been enough toilets for people to use. The second part of the problem has had social and cultural dimensions, including beliefs by some that it was unhygienic to have toilets inside the home.[17]

It is an issue of immense practical importance, but not one that is necessarily easy to talk about in political campaigns. In 2014, that changed in India. The election that year saw a new prime minister installed when Narendra Modi led his Hindu-nationalist BJP party to victory. Modi ran a campaign with an unexpectedly wide policy focus that incorporated some very practical issues, including discussing the issue of sanitation. In a soundbite that stuck, he argued that India needed 'toilets before temples'. He returned to that theme in his first Independence Day speech as prime minister in August 2014. He did not shy away from discussing this most 'basic' of issues on one of India's most important national days.

> Brother and Sisters, we are living in [the] 21st century. Has it ever pained us that our mothers and sisters have to defecate in [the] open? Whether [the] dignity of

women is not our collective responsibility? The poor womenfolk of the village wait for the night; until darkness descends, they can't go out to defecate. What bodily torture they must be feeling, how many diseases that act might engender. Can't we just make arrangements for toilets for the dignity of our mothers and sisters? . . . I come from a poor family, I have seen poverty. The poor need respect and it begins with cleanliness.[18]

Here was a narrative designed to tell a number of stories. The first was to underline that Modi wanted to differentiate himself from past prime ministers. He sought to position himself as different to the elites; as someone who understood the ordinary challenges of Indian life. It was an unapologetically populist message. But it also worked to shift the message on sanitation issues by portraying those left with no choice but to defecate in the open as the victims of a system that was letting them down. Modi was able to present the issue as a moral call to action – as a way for Indians to support their own families and communities by supporting the construction of toilets. Instead of haranguing people for not using toilets, the government message was promising to rescue people from an issue not of their creation. The data and evidence were clear that in a country of 1.2 billion people, hundreds of millions did not have proper access to a toilet.

Here was a clearly defined problem, a powerful narrative to push it forward, and no shortage of evidence to convince audiences at both domestic and international level that action was warranted. The fourth factor needed, of course, was to choose the right policy intervention. What could a government, faced with a country where half the population needed proper sanitation facilities, actually do? The answer was remarkably simple, even whilst the implementation would be incredibly complex. The answer was literally to build toilets. And not on some small scale. This was not to be a pilot programme. The goal was set to make India free from open defecation. Over one hundred million toilets would be required.

Building toilets, and then making sure they are used, has proven to be an immense undertaking. Many studies and commentaries have pointed to the complexities involved, and indeed to the excesses in the way the policy has been put into effect. There are allegations of drones being used to see if people are defecating outside, and of blocking access to some government services unless proof is provided that there is a toilet at home.[19] Many criticisms have emerged of Modi's approach, amid claims of intimidation and violence being used to force compliance, and of new forms of social ostracism.[20] At its most extreme, a case emerged in 2019 of two young children allegedly being killed simply for having been found defecating outside.[21]

Modi's stated policy goal had been to make India 'open defecation free' within five years. In October 2019, amidst much fanfare, he announced that India had achieved that goal. There is considerable evidence to suggest that this declaration of success may have been premature.[22] What is not in dispute is that Modi's programme has been successful in getting toilets built by the millions, and there is little doubt that the situation as regards open defecation has improved dramatically since 2014.

In terms of the politics of policymaking, Modi has been

able to get his ducks in a row. Once again, that does not mean that criticisms over his approach are not valid and disturbing – they are both. Many concerns have been expressed that success on the issue has come at the expense of the human rights of those who did not fall into line. Those concerns contributed to the Bill and Melinda Gates Foundation facing a backlash for conferring a 'Global Goalkeeper Award' on the prime minister in 2019.

Nevertheless, analysing the politics is about understanding why this project has been able to be framed as such a success. It began because Modi defined a practical problem that could be addressed by public policy after years of insufficient action. He built a narrative of moral imperative around the issue that could motivate and reach wide sections of the community. Rather than blaming people, at least initially, it was an appeal to every family to help look after the welfare of women and girls by doing something as 'simple' as building a toilet. He shaped a picture of himself as someone willing to tackle formerly taboo topics because he was a man of the people rather than a member of the elite. The first part of the intervention was so clear: build toilets. Lots of them. The second part, to then encourage their use and maintenance, has proved more difficult. But getting the four ducks into alignment gave Modi the chance to win the politics of policymaking on the issue, a chance which he has seized as one of his signature achievements.

Winter in Iceland is not just cold, but dark. Very dark. Close to the solstice in December, the daylight can offer you fewer than three hours' respite before the sun sets again. One of the few benefits is that this leaves plenty of time to enjoy the phenomenon of the northern lights, silhouetted against that night sky. All that is required is to get away from the artificial light of the city and head out to one of the many spectacular outdoor viewing sights.

The other thing needed is time to really soak up the experience. Whether sitting in some hot springs and looking skywards, or camping out with the family, this surely promises to be something special. But the public policy issue I'm getting at here is not about the night sky itself; it is about having the time to look at it.

What if the government could legislate to give you some of that time you desperately crave? You might spend it looking at the northern lights, or you might decide to curl up at home with a good book in front of a warm fire. The choice is yours, but only if government policy decides to give you that choice.

In Iceland, the government has been looking at ways to do exactly that. It wants to give its citizens more time for themselves in the hope that it will make them happier. Between 2015 and 2019, the government combined with Reykjavik City Council to trial shorter working hours for the same pay. In what has become known as the 'four-day week', thousands of workers had their normal hours shortened from forty hours to thirty-five or thirty-six hours during this pilot scheme. It may not sound like much, but researchers who studied the effects noticed significant changes. A report by the think tank 'Autonomy' and the Association for Sustainability and Democracy suggested many positives.[23] Whilst productivity didn't drop, and in fact improved in some instances, 'worker well-being increased across a range of indicators, from perceived stress and burnout, to health and work-life balance.'[24] Not surprisingly, these findings caught the world's attention. Mainstream news outlets across the globe reported on the success of the trial.

It's still early days on this initiative, and the politics of policymaking can change fast. But for the moment, the Icelandic government and Reykjavik City Council have worked hard to get their ducks in a row. As always that starts with a clear understanding of the problem they're trying to solve. In some senses, the problem is simply that Iceland works too hard in ways that come at a high personal cost for its citizens. The problem was framed from the outset not in traditionally narrow economic terms, but in the wider sense of 'well-being' as a holistic idea. The data suggest that Iceland has traditionally had the longest working hours of the Scandinavian countries. As a result, it performs relatively poorly in surveys on work-life balance. So, when looking for potential policy interventions, policymakers started by exploring the idea that working five days a week is not necessarily the best way to achieve maximum human happiness and productivity.

The narrative around this sits comfortably within a wider Icelandic government agenda to move away from measuring wealth only by traditional indicators like GDP, and to embrace instead a much wider set of criteria. Prime Minister Katrín Jakobsdóttir, speaking at Chatham House in London in December 2019, argued that a well-being approach requires investment in social infrastructure, a better work-life balance, mental health support and cleaner energy solutions.[25] Whilst not specifically mentioning the four-day week, the tenor was clear: Iceland was going to measure things differently from now on.

Enter the four-day week. Here is a potential policy intervention that is tailor-made to fit with the problem, the data on long working hours in Iceland, and the narrative about the need for a greater emphasis on well-being. The report published by Autonomy refers to multiple academic studies supporting the proposition that a reduction in working hours leads to numerous well-being benefits without seeing a drop in productivity. That is certainly what seems to have happened in Iceland. So favourable were the findings of the trials that shorter working hours have now been made official across Iceland's economy, through deals between the major unions, the government, and local councils. To quote the report: 'This means that 86 per cent of Iceland's entire working population has now either moved to working shorter hours or have had new mechanisms made available to them through which they can negotiate shorter hours in their workplace.'[26]

The ducks are in a row. Once again, that does not mean there is not challenge from critics. Multiple scholars have come forward since the report came out to essentially pull back the reins a little on the galloping enthusiasm of news outlets that had declared the four-day week to be an unmitigated success. Critics have correctly pointed out that cutting four hours off the working week is not actually the same as declaring a 'four-day week'.[27] Indeed, the Icelandic agreements to now reduce working hours right across the country apparently equate to as little as thirty-five fewer minutes a week for some private sector workers.[28]

Nonetheless, the success of the programme so far shows that winning at the politics of policymaking doesn't necessarily mean winning on each of the smaller details. If the ducks are in a row, the nuances can tend to wash out in favour of sweeping narratives and headline analysis of interventions. The world now believes, for better or worse, that Icelanders will work a four-day week from here on in.[29] That is a powerful piece of politics that has the capacity to resonate well beyond Iceland. Plenty of research on policy learning and policy exchange shows how quickly policy ideas spread to other parts of the world. We have not heard the last of the four-day week, and not just in Iceland.

'Dear Tony . . .' So began the letter. The Tony in question was the director general of the BBC, Tony Hall. The signatories to the letter were a long list of some of the BBC's biggest stars, writing to the boss of their organization in 2017. What these stars had in common was that they were all women. The subject of the letter was the fact that a list of the BBC's top earners had just been released, confirming people's worst fears about the gender pay gap within the organization. As the letter noted, all the women who signed it acknowledged that they were fortunate to have great jobs that paid well. But that wasn't the issue. The issue was that 'women at the BBC are being paid less than men for the same work.'[30]

The gender pay gap is not new. All too many women are all too well aware of just how depressingly 'old' that pay gap actually is. What is perhaps slightly newer is that we are at least now talking about it. The public conversation has shifted away from unconvincing attempts to justify the gender pay gap towards pledges to do better. It's a policy problem that is certainly not unique to either the BBC or to the UK as a whole. Very few countries on earth have a good story to tell on the gender pay gap. The most thoughtful on the topic have once again been some of the Scandinavian countries, which have also been the most active in trying to address the issue.

Just how can we define this problem? It is both simple and complex. The simple part is that women are being paid less than men. The complex part is that the reasons for it are a combination of interlinked failings. The research points to aspects such as: women being concentrated in sectors that are less well recompensed as a whole; women being more likely to see breaks in their career for family or caring reasons (meaning they fall behind male peers on the climb up the slippery ladder of seniority); and negotiated individual pay contracts in which women are offered less than men.[31] It has proved difficult for governments to split and target each of these factors in effective ways.

The UK government, in line with many of its European counterparts, has recently focused in on the last component – the lack of transparency around the pay differential. If women are not aware that men in the same organization are getting paid considerably more, it makes change less likely. It is hard to negotiate for more if you don't know how much more is actually possible. It is self-evidently only one part of the puzzle, but it has enabled governments to at least get a grip on a distinct part of the problem.

The most obvious solution for breaking through darkness is sunlight. The only way that women could know what their male counterparts were being paid would be if that data was made public. So that is what the UK government decided to do. Although plans for reporting of the gender pay gap were first legislated in the 2010 Equalities Act, the Conservative government initially chose to make enforcement of this a voluntary process. Companies would be encouraged rather than forced into the release of information. Perhaps unsurprisingly, only a handful of large companies went to the time and effort to release information on an issue that was unlikely to reflect well on them. A flawed intervention based on asking companies to essentially 'out themselves' as poor performers was never likely to work. By 2015, the Cameron government was ready to acknowledge that compulsion would be needed.

A clear narrative was set out by the PM, and the then minister for Women and Equalities, Nicky Morgan, on why action was warranted. They framed it as a matter of economic importance as well as a fairness measure. In the words of Nicky Morgan: 'This is not just the right thing to do, it makes good business sense: supporting women to fulfil their potential could increase the size of our economy by 35 per cent.'[32] Prime Minister Cameron penned an opinion piece in *The Times*, first reminding readers that all parents have the same common goals for their children. 'As a father of two daughters, I want them to experience complete gender equality in the workplace when they start their careers.'[33] He acknowledged that 'overall, a woman still earns just 80p for every £1 earned by a man. That is a scandal – and I'm determined to close the gap.' This was then buttressed by further commitments to 'help more women reach the top' and to work towards more affordable childcare to make it easier for women to rejoin the workforce after having children if they chose to.

At least temporarily, the government got its ducks in a row. By defining the problem as one of 'transparency', policymakers opened up new avenues for action. Governments have the levers available to force the publication of information in a way that others can't. Government is good at compulsion within a narrow range (not that this is always well received!). Companies and organizations that had been able to keep their record secret suddenly found themselves embarrassed on a very public stage.

Each year, as the updated evidence is released, multiple critical media stories now follow. Companies are named and shamed for their poor records. High-profile women are able to take their organizations to task about their data. Without needing to mandate that companies actually *do something* concrete to change the situation, government has nonetheless succeeded in shaming them into *some* action. The reputational damage is too much for organizations to simply turn their back and say they don't care. The publicity is too great and the potential of losing outstanding women employees has become a very real danger.

That is not to say that government has solved the gender pay gap issue. Far from it. The gap persists, and the Covid pandemic has in fact made it worse in many organizations. The UK government has also been criticized for the low level of specificity it requires from organizations, its slackness in chasing up companies that don't lodge their data, and the lack of effective follow-up on the information that is provided. What is more, having introduced the change, the government has kicked a series of own goals on the issue during the pandemic, suspending the reporting requirement at a time when the evidence suggests things have been getting considerably worse.

It is another reminder that policy doesn't stand still, and that ducks can break ranks very quickly. A temporary political success in addressing the issue led to a welcome raising of awareness about it. Companies that may not have actively thought about addressing the gender pay gap in the past have been forced to do so now. The task for the UK government, as for others around the world, is to make sure that the transparency sticks, whilst moving to address the other factors that are stopping the gap from closing. It is one thing for governments to make people notice the gap is there, and quite another to actually make it disappear.

That includes in organizations like the BBC, which has worked hard in recent years to convince critics that it is serious about tackling the issue. That began with a direct reply from Tony Hall to that letter from more than forty of the BBC's most high-profile women. He pledged that the BBC would close the gap altogether by 2020 (earlier if possible), and pointed to improvements that had already been made in the gender balance amongst presenters. The data suggest that in 2020 a gender pay gap still exists at the BBC, albeit one that has shrunk from 2017 levels. The challenge continues.

What this chapter shows is that when all four factors do align, policymaking suddenly looks easier. Each of the ducks plays a part in mobilizing a particular aspect of community support to make sure that changes get through. That's what leads to success. Getting the problem definition right means that stakeholders, interest groups and the wider public are nodding along. As Labour Shadow Home Secretary in the early 1990s, Tony Blair famously set out a formulation on what the party's position would be on tackling crime: they would be 'tough on crime and tough on the causes of crime'. In addition to being a great slogan and a powerful opening line for a policy story, this also played the role of a high-level piece of problem definition. It let listeners know that crime is not just about the weak personal morals of individuals who can't help themselves from coveting their neighbours' property. It is also a social problem that has causes that governments can address. Whether the policy interventions actually put in place when Blair got into government were the right ones for meeting that problem is less clear. But the first duck definitely fell into line.

If the problem is clearly defined, the right narrative can then win wider political support. It gives politicians something to sell to their constituents – a good story to tell when they're slapping backs and shaking hands in their local pub. The story will be changed and delivered in different ways at the local level, but if the narrative has done its job, then people will be able to connect to the story. Making that align with the data and evidence is what's necessary to mobilize the think tanks, scientists, scholars and civil servants who deal in data and evidence to also jump on board. Often derided as elites, it is the capacity of this group to start writing favourable op-eds, initiate research projects, and talk on the airwaves that gives vital impetus to any intervention that is actually adopted. They provide the details that turn what is so far just a good story into something more compelling.

Finally, getting the right intervention in place means the other three ducks have not aligned in vain. Without the right intervention, the policy process finds itself all dressed up with nowhere to go. Community support has been mobilized, the elite knowledge brokers have been harnessed, and constituents are confirming that the problem definition passes the 'pub test'. The 'wrong' intervention not only dissipates that energy but, worse, can potentially channel it back against the government that has promised so much only to deliver so little. But getting the right policy intervention is really hard. There are complex interactions and unintended consequences to consider. If you choose to legalize drugs or prostitution in response to the problems they cause, will that lead to other problems? The short answer is yes: any intervention will have knock-on effects.

Getting all four ducks in alignment is powerful. Political and policy success beckons. But there are also many examples of governments thinking that they have their ducks in a row, only to find that success still eludes them. Sometimes, in politics, you just lose. But look closer, and you see that all too often the loss is because the ducks were not actually in line to begin with.

6. When the Ducks Don't Swim, Look Harder

If you are lucky enough to have visited the town of Broome on the north-west coast of Western Australia, you'll know why so many celebrities flock there for holiday breaks. Cable Beach, once one of the world's best-kept secrets, is now a tourism hotspot. Vast sands look out towards the never-ending waters of the Indian Ocean. There are of course drawbacks too. It has been known for very large saltwater crocodiles to pop up occasionally on Cable Beach, but let's not spoil the mood.

Even by the standards of a big continent, the state of Western Australia is a vast place. It is ten times the size of the UK. Its coastline dwarfs that of most countries on earth, with over 20,000 kilometres of it to take in. Of course, not all of Western Australia looks like Cable Beach. Alongside coastal holiday towns, there are also several larger coastal centres – the ports that bring people and goods to and from parts of this enormous state. One of the biggest is the town of Port Hedland, about six hundred kilometres south of Broome.

Port Hedland is in some ways a curious place. It's a boom town, but of a particular type. It's not some kind of Las Vegas of glitz and glamour. It is a gritty, earthy, mining town and port. It is the end point for the materials dug out of the ground across the vast Pilbara mining region. Pull out a map of Australia and you'll get a sense of just how large an area this is, and just how remote a centre Port Hedland is.

As I write this book, Port Hedland is on a trajectory out of boom times. That doesn't mean it's going bust, just that the normal madness is subsiding slightly. Read through some of the many media stories about the town and you'll get a sense of what the boom actually looked like. A Bloomberg piece by Krystal Chia captures it perfectly: 'In one of the most remote corners of the Earth, its real estate was more expensive than in Manhattan, service workers earned bankers' salaries, and its small airport began running direct flights to Bali, where miners bought beach houses to relax between stints in the red-stained Pilbara hills.'[1]

You get the picture. Many a British miner coping with the bitter realities of coalpit closures in Thatcher's Britain in the 1980s would be entitled to shake their head. As they know only too well, boom times don't last for ever. Growing awareness of the environmental price to be paid – including in the red mining dust that coats Port Hedland – now looms larger too.

Mining has never just been about jobs. Mining is a way of life for whole communities. It's about the dignity of work, even in the face of the regular searing tragedies of lives lost underground. Tradition, family connections, and emotional roots loom large in mining communities across the globe. For too many mining towns in the past fifty years, their story has been very different to Port Hedland's. Their reality has been one of decline. Squeezed wages, falling commodity prices, and a degree of corporate greed have all played a role. The causes are complex and multifarious, but the results are depressingly similar. From the Welsh valleys in Britain, to the coalfields of Pennsylvania in the USA, the past five decades have seen pit closures and conflict. Fierce resistance from communities determined to protect their way of life is hardly surprising.

Mining has always been a boom-and-bust industry. Commodity prices go up and down and recessions can be brutal for small towns. So when the booms are on, they have to be squeezed hard to yield every bit of available benefit. When mining towns are doing well, it is a reality of economic life that the mining companies who run them are doing even better. It is no coincidence that some of the biggest, wealthiest corporations on the globe are natural resources companies.

Mining has traditionally been one of the cornerstones of Australia's economic success. It showed its strength and resilience in particular during the worldwide meltdown of the late 2000s that we know as the Global Financial Crisis (GFC). Most readers will remember all too readily the devastating impacts of this catastrophe across the globe. Governments suddenly had to do things once seen as unthinkable. The Bush administration in the US and the Brown government in the UK bailed out financial institutions to the tune of billions of dollars overnight. Faced with the complete meltdown of the financial sector, governments everywhere did what they could to stem the bleeding. Even then, the economic impacts were brutal. Britain went into recession in 2008 and stayed there for over a year. The economy shrank by over 6 per cent. Unemployment reached 8.4 per cent. House prices tumbled and wages stagnated.[2]

Not so in Australia. As the rest of the world was reeling in the face of forces no single government could control, Australia somehow dodged the bullet. While almost every other advanced economy dug deeper into recession, Australia's economy didn't go into recession at all. While unemployment rates doubled around the globe, in Australia they went up by less than 2 percentage points and stayed at under 6 per cent throughout.

There remains deep contestation in Australian politics about why the country pulled through the GFC so well. The Labor government, under Prime Minister Kevin Rudd, acted swiftly at the start of the crisis by pumping billions into the economy through direct cash grants to households, building projects and other items. Exports to China also played a part. And the biggest exports were those from the mining industry. As China pursued its own building programme to counteract the impacts of the GFC, Australia was one of the beneficiaries. It sent its commodities to China on an ever-increasing scale. Port Hedland prospered as the ships lined up to take away the spoils.

Whilst the world went bust, Australia experienced a mining boom. It was good for jobs, good for the economy, and good for those mining companies. Unsurprisingly, the Rudd government decided this was a good time to start a national conversation about the rate of tax being paid by the big miners. There was widespread political acquiescence that there might be room for improvement. Such was the extent of the riches pouring in that even the mining companies themselves were open to the idea of paying a little more.

So the problem definition here wasn't really about a problem at all, so much as how best to distribute the unexpectedly vast wealth being wrung from Australia's natural resource sector. The government's narrative followed accordingly. The rhetoric was focused on presenting the iron ore coming out of the ground as a public asset – a common good in the literal sense – which rightly belonged to all Australians. It was also a non-renewable good, because it could literally only be dug up out of the ground once. The Australian people were entitled to a greater share of the largesse flowing from the sale of public assets.

The government worked hard to make sure the data and evidence lined up. They had commissioned a two-year review of the entire Australian taxation system. You know a review is serious when the words 'root and branch' make their way into the conversation. This was a piece of work that would look at the whole system to paint a picture of the most efficient and fair taxation regime for twenty-first century Australia. The review was to be chaired by the Permanent Secretary to the Treasury, Ken Henry, whose name quickly became synonymous with it.

The review was as deep and wide as its remit suggested. Set up in 2008, prior to the GFC, the review conferred widely with all the expected stakeholder groups, and released consultation papers as it went. It held public meetings in every Australian capital city and followed up with focus groups.[3] The review delivered its final report in December 2009, complete with 138 recommendations set within its 783 pages.

The problem for a government that commissions a root-and-branch tax review is that it might get one! That is exactly what happened here. Prime Minister Rudd and his Treasurer Wayne Swan were handed a document which they viewed as a potential policy hand grenade. The nation's finances looked very different in December 2009 than they had in May 2008 when the review had begun. The GFC had seen to that. The national conversation had changed. The government's wider popularity had also declined. There was not much political appetite, less than a year from an election, to spend long days talking about taxation. What to do? The government spent the next four or five months sitting on the report whilst deciding how best to respond.

When the response came in May 2010, it zeroed in specifically on one main recommendation – the creation of what would be called the 'Resource Super Profits Tax'. Colloquially it became known simply as the mining tax. To be introduced in 2012, the tax would be aimed at the so-called 'super-profits' of mining companies, with 40 per cent of those 'super-profits' intended to come to government coffers.

Surely this looks like alignment – like a government that has got its ducks in a row. There's a clear problem, and it's a 'good' problem to have, which is that mining is booming and there is an opportunity for more public money to be raised. The evidence base is strong. No one disputed that the mining companies were in fact making extraordinary profits, and no one could say that the Henry Tax Review had not been thorough. The narrative was clear and powerful. What politician anywhere in the world wouldn't like to point the finger at big business 'unfairly' taking more than its fair share? The fact that mineral resources are an irreplaceable public good just made the case stronger. The final duck was the intervention, which was targeted and carefully calibrated to only pull in the 'super-profits' rather than trying to put mining companies out of business. The ducks were aligned. The music was playing. Surely this was a home run?

It is hard to convey just how spectacularly this thing went wrong. Instead of running into an open goal, the government ran into a brick wall. What should have been a policy triumph instead became a policy millstone. There was a backlash from mining companies, negative opinion polls and a rampant opposition with an uncompromising new leader in Tony Abbott. Within weeks, Prime Minister Rudd had been dumped by his own party, with the mining tax seen as one of the biggest contributing factors. How could this have gone so badly?

When you look hard, you find that the government had convinced itself that its ducks were in a row when the reverse was actually true. The alignment was a mirage. It had not won the battle of problem definition at the outset, nor constructed a strong enough narrative to support its agenda. The government needed to fundamentally convince Australians that there was something wrong with the mining industry doing this well without paying more tax. They fumbled that ball. There was no groundswell of community outrage at the proceeds of the mining boom not being shared.

It is also clear that the government was overwhelmed by the ferocity with which the mining companies were willing to fight the proposed tax changes. Having initially been open to the conversation, the government's missteps and the changing events opened up opportunities for resistance that the companies could exploit. Most importantly, they were able to construct a counter-narrative to the government's own. Painted by ministers as taking more than their fair share, the miners set out a different story.

In a quite extraordinary PR blitz, opponents of the mining tax unleashed a blizzard of television and newspaper advertisements presenting mining companies as partners in building Australian communities. These were good ads. There were ads telling the story of individuals who'd been given the chance to do amazing jobs, talking to camera, watching them at work. Engineers, tech experts, energy experts and more. There were ads focused on the social contribution, showing all the facets of a community working in harmony, supported and sponsored by mining companies. Sports teams, charities at work, iconic-looking Australians silhouetted against blue skies and red dirt – all came daily to Australia's television screens and newspapers. The message from the mining companies was simple: we sit at the heart of Australian life. We are a part of the community, not some great behemoth looking to rip off Australians. It was a masterful piece of storytelling. It also hit its target in only a matter of weeks.

When the government first announced the mining tax at the start of May 2010, things were looking good. Initial media coverage suggested this looked like a winning political strategy. There were predictions that it would boost the Rudd government's popularity ahead of the election expected later in the year. How cruel politics can be. In Western Australia, home to Port Hedland and to large parts of Australia's mining industry, the opinion polling tells the story. The Roy Morgan polling company undertook a series of weekly polls during May 2010. When the mining tax was unveiled at the start of May, disapproval in this very pro-mining state was at 54 per cent amongst voters. Within three weeks, that number was at 78 per cent.[4]

Nationally, the polls told a similar story. For much of its first two years in office, the Rudd government had enjoyed an almost unbelievable level of support in the polls. Through major policy announcements in areas as diverse as industrial relations reform, an apology to the Stolen Generations of Indigenous children, and the swift response to the GFC, the government looked as though it could do no wrong. When sworn into office in December 2007, various opinion polls showed that support for Rudd's Labor Party was in the 57–61 per cent range, compared to the opposition, which was languishing somewhere between 38 and 43 per cent of the two-party preferred vote. That was reflected too in the standing of the prime minister. One poll showed Rudd as having 70 per cent approval as preferred prime minister; stratospheric stuff by Australian political standards.[5]

This didn't shift much for the next two years. The opposition burned through a succession of leaders and, when it landed on Tony Abbott in December 2009, Rudd was still running at 60 per cent as preferred prime minister to Abbott's 23 per cent, with Labor ahead by big margins. Yet six months later, by June 2010, all bets were off. Abbott had cut dramatically into Rudd's lead as preferred PM, and more importantly the gap between the parties had narrowed sharply. One poll had it dead even at 50 per cent of the vote each, whereas others showed a narrow lead for Labor.[6]

The government was politically outplayed by the sheer relentlessness of the mining industry and a rejuvenated and combative political opposition led by Tony Abbott. The mining tax brought to a head simmering issues running beneath the surface in the Labor Party, where there was deep unhappiness amongst some Labor MPs with Rudd's internal leadership style. The endgame saw Rudd unceremoniously dumped in what remains one of the most extraordinary forty-eight hours in the recent history of Australian politics. Having initially agreed to a leadership contest for 24 June, Rudd instead resigned when he gauged that the numbers would have seen him defeated in the party room vote. Julia Gillard succeeded him as prime minister.

One of Gillard's first acts as leader was to reshape the proposed Resource Super Profits Tax after holding talks with the big mining companies. This was the final recognition that the fourth duck – the policy intervention of the mining tax itself – was out of kilter. Under Gillard's leadership, the tax rate was reduced, it was renamed the Minerals Resources Rent Tax, and all in all the government was pleased just to be able to get the debate off the table. 'We've been stuck on this question as a nation for too long,' Gillard said when announcing the deal.[7] Surrounded by the political carnage after weeks at war with the resources sector, few in her own party would have disagreed.

The mining tax debate in Australia provides a salutary lesson on the nature of political power. Power is never absolute, even in apparent autocracies, let alone democracies. In democratic countries, the range of people and interests that can challenge a policy agenda is vast. Policy success is never guaranteed. The four ducks do not align simply because the government believes that they should.

Beyond the political factors, some problems are also notoriously knotty. Many social problems have so many interlocking parts that the complexity overwhelms attempts to fix them. At best it becomes possible to 'manage' them by attacking just one aspect at a time. Like a game of whack-a-mole, the problem doesn't sit still while governments work through it. These problems, labelled 'wicked problems' by policy scholars, have dealt a heavy blow to many a political career. Health issues, crime, poverty and homelessness, to name but a few, fit into this classification.

The issue of obesity belongs in the same category. The UK has a weight problem. Data has increasingly shown not just that large numbers of people are overweight or obese, but that the problem has been getting progressively worse. So why don't governments act? The truth is that they are trying. Over the course of the last thirty years, there have been multiple policy strategies launched by both Conservative and Labour governments in the UK. The problem is clear, the data and evidence are undisputed, the political narrative has long confirmed that this is a problem, and we've had thirty years of policy action. Yet, none of that has made a significant dent in this seemingly insoluble problem. Why?

Cue the scene. It's Christmas. The season of goodwill. The time to get together and see loved ones who you've missed throughout the year. People across the country drive long distances to be with their families. This year it might be the grandparents' turn to host. The front door is thrown open after your tentative knock. What are the first words you hear? 'You've been living rather well,' says grandma, looking you up and down and giving you a poke in the stomach. 'Are you exercising, are you eating right?' You refrain from pointing out to grandma that she herself could be said to be carrying a few pounds. Instead, you say 'Happy Christmas' and leave it at that.

Even if grandma's observation is correct, whose fault is it? What actually is the problem here? Well, it could indeed be that we're not 'eating right', as she says, meaning that we're consuming too many fatty foods and sugars and not enough of the healthy stuff. We could probably also do with taking a bit more exercise, that's true. So, grandma's not necessarily wrong, but she is only revealing one corner of the actual problem.

Millions of people in Britain live below the poverty line. Millions more find themselves in the 'just getting by' category. Fresh, healthy food is expensive. For people living on low incomes, small amounts can mean the difference between getting a meal on the table or not. And that's any meal, let alone one with the right balance of food groups and calories. Food poverty is a very real issue, highlighted to such extraordinary effect by the Manchester United footballer Marcus Rashford in his public lobbying of the government to continue to provide free school meals during the Covid crisis. If the difference is between eating and not eating, then sophisticated government messages about eating *well* don't really come into the equation.

As already mentioned, grandma herself is also carrying a few pounds. That matters. Genetics do influence the challenges individuals face with maintaining a healthy weight. The medical evidence shows that some people are more genetically prone to obesity than others, and therefore face a tougher fight to prevent it. Upbringing joins in as a further factor. In so many aspects of life, we replicate our own upbringing. So, if we didn't eat wonderfully healthy meals as youngsters, it's more likely that we'll continue those patterns into adulthood.

Then there is the physical and mental health side. Being overweight can make some people feel miserable. And what do we do when we feel miserable? Well, comfort food isn't a bad start. Of course, we all know we won't cure our anger at being overweight by consuming a tub of ice cream, but at least it makes us feel better for a few hours. Psychological trauma, 'fat-shaming' behaviour and the relentless pressure on the young in particular to meet various physical stereotypes of perfection based on current fashions also pile into the mix.

So what's the problem? Pretty much everything's the problem! Rude comments from grandma, poverty, psychological pressure, bad food, not enough exercise, insufficient transport alternatives to cars, genetics, bad upbringing, and unreal stereotypes of perfect bodies. Fix all of those things and you'll solve the obesity problem. Not much chance of that.

This is a classic example of a 'wicked' problem. There is no one single issue that causes people to become overweight. Rather, there are a set of interrelated factors that are incredibly hard to untangle. Emotional issues, cultural norms, family problems, financial pressures, health challenges, genetic predisposition and 'bad' behavioural choices all play a part. Success would require a whole flotilla of ducks swimming simultaneously and in synchronized ways. Few governments have the time, power or focus to make that happen.

What governments have had to do is have a go at the issues individually rather than collectively, meaning they are never actually able to solve the whole problem. Most commonly on obesity policy, this has seen the focus placed on diet and exercise as the two pieces of the puzzle that government might be most likely to successfully target. The choice of narrative has been interesting. In the case of something like smoking, it was relatively easy for governments to lay the blame at the feet of 'big tobacco' for leading vulnerable people astray. Addicted people were portrayed as victims of the allegedly immoral behaviour of these companies. Generally speaking, that has proved harder to do when combating obesity levels. Fast-food and soft-drink companies have been targeted with advertising restrictions, for example, but it has not been possible to portray food manufacturers as the knowing purveyors of evil in the same way that big tobacco was targeted.

Whilst the health problems associated with obesity are acute, they are perhaps more varied than their tobacco-induced counterparts. Governments, and the health experts who advise them, have been able to draw a direct line from smoking to lung cancer in linear fashion. With obesity, the evidence base showing poor health effects cannot be doubted, but it is harder to paint with the same degree of clarity. An increased chance of developing diabetes, extra strain on joints, some emerging links to cancer, etc. – the possibilities are so many in number and so complex that it's harder to drive the message home. The narrative in the end revolves around 'feeling better' in any number of ways. Whilst that's enough to motivate many individuals, as a message it cannot compete for clarity with statements like 'smoking causes mouth and throat cancer' (which has appeared on Australian cigarette packets).

As a result, the interventions adopted to improve obesity

rates suffer from a similar lack of precision. They essentially try to cajole people into 'better' behaviours. If only it were that easy. An excellent recent study by Cambridge researchers Dolly Theis and Martin White assessed obesity policies in England stretching back over the last thirty years. The study identified no less than fourteen separate strategies to tackle obesity in that time, under both Conservative and Labour governments. Why, after thirty years of action, has nothing changed? Theis and White conclude that it is because the interventions chosen aren't effective and that the implementation regimes around them are poor. That is compounded by a lack of institutional memory, which means each new strategy adopts measures disappointingly similar to the last, only to see the same disappointing results.[8] Simply cajoling and encouraging individuals to improve their diets and exercise hasn't worked.

Obesity policy shows again that when the ducks appear to be in a row, but success remains elusive, we need to look harder. On closer inspection, the ducks on obesity policy are out of line. The problem definition remains too contested – between being a problem of poor personal choices and being a systemic failure that governments can and should address. As a result, narratives get caught up in 'nanny state' politics, leading to intervention options that don't match the complexity of the problem.

Politically, governments don't seem to have suffered much electoral damage for not solving the obesity crisis. No UK prime minister has been voted out of office for not forcing people to exercise more or taxing fast food at higher rates. Quite the opposite really. Governments have been unwilling to risk their political capital in forcing through potentially unpopular policies to dramatically increase the price of 'bad' foods. Politically, who can blame them? And social inequality also means that any attempt to do so would have an outsized impact on poorer families, who are struggling to cover the weekly food bill as it is. The ducks don't get in a row because the interventions are not equal to the task that is asked of them.

One of the most recent UK contributions to the conversation on ways to combat obesity was the National Food Strategy, commissioned by the Johnson government and produced under the leadership of Henry Dimbleby. It included proposals for a sugar and salt tax, formulated so as to incentivize food manufacturers to save money by putting less of these ingredients in their products. The prime minister's response was that he was 'not attracted to the idea of extra taxes on hard working people'.[9] The fate of the Danish fat tax acts as a warning of what can go wrong. Sometimes the politics just seem too hard.

In 2016 in Nevada something rather frightening happened. It wasn't a big-bang event, but a quiet harbinger of potentially unthinkable catastrophe. In September 2016, in Reno, a woman died in hospital of an infection. Sadly, of course, this kind of tragic event is not all that rare. People die in hospitals around the world every day. Grieving families are left to grapple with the emotional aftermath while the world continues on around them. What made this particular death frightening on a wider scale is that there were no medicines capable of preventing it. The infection which took this woman's life could not be stopped because there was literally no antibiotic available in the United States capable of overcoming it. It was a superbug – one of the emerging strains of bacteria which scientists have been warning us about for many years. Too often those warnings have fallen on disbelieving ears because in the end there has always still been an antibiotic capable of fighting back. There has always been a shield.

In September 2016 that shield wall was breached. All twenty-six legally registered antibiotics were tested against the bug and all twenty-six were found wanting. The tragic case of this one woman was a reminder of the wider potential tragedy yet to come. She is not the first person in the world to have died from a superbug, but her case illustrated starkly that the most advanced medical system in the developed world did not have a single antibiotic capable of saving her life. How could the government have let that situation happen?

As always, the answer is complicated. It's not as if the American government has ever just waved the white flag in the face of the superbug threat. Quite the opposite, actually. It has put in place a series of perfectly defensible policy strategies to tackle this slow-burning threat.

The story – the policy narrative – is a powerful one. It's quite possible that it will now seem even more potent against the backdrop of the Covid pandemic, which has surely shaken our certainty in the limitless power of modern medicine. It centres on driving home just how much we rely on antibiotics in so many facets of human and animal medicine. Pretty much every patient who undergoes open surgery in our hospitals is given antibiotics as a precaution against infection. Without antibiotics that work, operations that are now considered standard and safe become immediately more high risk. But that is just the tip of an extremely large iceberg.

In 2014, President Obama signed an executive order on 'combating antibiotic resistant bacteria', setting up a taskforce with membership from across government to drive progress on the issue. Congress has shown bipartisan support, but differences remain, with the Trump administration supporting continued high use of antibiotics in various arms of agribusiness.[10] The Centres for Disease Control (CDC) in the United States released a major report into the spread and impact of antimicrobial resistance in 2013, and a second report in 2019. It doesn't pull its punches, confirming that there are over 2.8 million superbug infections in the US each year, linked to over 35,000 deaths.[11] The 'good' news, if it can be called that, is that this means the situation has improved slightly since the first 2013 report. But only slightly, and the threat from some bugs has grown dramatically. The report lists eighteen known superbugs as causes of major concern, ranked in order of the potential severity of their impacts.

So the data and evidence are clear. The added complication, of course, is that antimicrobial resistance is not just an American problem. It is global in scope. As Covid has so recently underlined, germs and viruses don't respect international borders. They jump around, mutate, and come back in ever stronger and more resistant forms.

The interventions put in place in some ways have very little to do with medicine per se and much more to do with human behaviour. Put bluntly, we've all taken antibiotics for granted for too long. Such was their miraculous healing power that we've thrown them at everything we possibly can, unaware that in doing so we're diluting their future effectiveness. That includes feeding them to animals in the millions as a preventative medicine. It includes demanding them from our doctors for every possible human ailment, whether they're actually the right remedy or not. Their very existence has allowed us to be less scrupulous in dealing with skin scrapes and small wounds, secure in the knowledge that if we get an infection an antibiotic will be able to fight it off.

That's why the CDC report suggests that the way to combat this threat is through more careful behaviour. In hospitals, that means redoubling efforts to ensure that all equipment is thoroughly sterilized and that entry points for things like catheters don't become infection sites. If a superbug is detected, it's about making sure that patients are isolated quickly to avoid spread. Out in the community, it means support for vaccinations and screening to stop people getting sick in the first place. It means making sure food is handled carefully and with clean hands so bacteria cannot grab a hold. Following the Covid pandemic, such measures seem even less revolutionary than they did before.

Even with all those precautions, the experts know that we can't stop superbugs from evolving and challenging our existing antibiotics. In wonderfully evocative language, the CDC has labelled the worst of these as 'nightmare bacteria' – specifically referring to Carbapenem-Resistant Enterobacteriaceae (CRE), which can 'survive and grow in sink drains at health-care facilities and spread to patients and to the environment through the wastewater'.[12] With such lethal opponents to beat, part of the solution also needs to be the development of new, stronger antibiotics capable of beating new bugs as they emerge.

At first glance, the ducks seem to be in a row here. We have a laudably clear problem, with a straightforward story about the consequences if we let things go unchecked. Politicians in mainstream political parties on both sides of the aisle are on board in recognizing the problem, if not always agreeing on the response. The data and evidence have been built up with real rigour over the past decade, not just by the CDC but by similar national-level reports around the world. And there are solutions being put into place. Doctors are being more careful about when they prescribe antibiotics. The agricultural sector is trying to limit the amount of antibiotics being put in things like cattle feed as a routine additive. Hospitals have clear procedures in place for preventing spread.

The issue here is that the current interventions are too tame for the existential nature of the problem. There has been no new class of antibiotics developed since the 1980s. A 2016 British report on the issue cast this as partly an economics problem.[13] To put it starkly, pharmaceutical companies don't make much money from new antibiotics compared to new drugs to treat something like cancer. Producing new antibiotics is a high-cost, research-intensive activity in order to produce a low-cost, wide-use product that will quickly be turned into generic brands once monopoly IP protection for them runs out. In other words, the economic incentives are wrong.

So the fourth duck is out of line with the seriousness of the challenge. The problem definition, the narrative, and the available data all tell us that we are heading for a day of reckoning for modern medicine. The policy intervention – the fourth duck – suggests that we can beat it by just being a bit more careful in what we do with antibiotics. It's a start, but governments are deluding themselves if they think it's enough. Like those Hollywood disaster movies in which a meteor is headed towards Earth, we know these superbugs are coming. Even if we launch everything we have at them, we might still miss. But in a way that has similarities to the current climate-change challenge, governments need to do more to get their ducks in a row. The narrative in both cases points to looming catastrophe, whilst the policy solutions presented are only 'steady as she goes' at best. The ducks are out of line.

As already noted, crime is a wicked problem. It never really goes away. Criminologists help us understand it, and governments fight to decrease it, but societies without crime are the stuff of science-fiction fantasy rather than earthly reality. Politically, crime remains one of the most keenly contested ideological battlefields on the public policy landscape. Centre-right parties the world over are famed for their 'getting tough on crime' initiatives. They frequently find themselves accused ahead of each election of playing the 'law-and-order' card as they settle on the latest compilation of increased sentences and tougher policing. The same arguments in reverse plague left-of-centre governments, who find themselves accused of being soft on crime, as they are seen to focus more on re-habilitation than punishment as the main policy priority.

The debate has also increasingly manifested itself in economic terms. Crime is undoubtedly a public problem, but there has been less consensus on whether that means it should also have a public solution. Take something like prisons. Should prisons be privatized, or does the potential intrusion of a profit motive into the incarceration of human beings introduce too many complexities? Right-of-centre parties traditionally have a preference for market solutions. Saving public money whilst getting things done more efficiently seems like such a clear benefit. Left-of-centre parties are more likely to point out that markets aren't necessarily designed for taking good care of people who don't necessarily conform to the input-and-output models of market economics.

It is a perennial debate. One of its latest iterations in the UK centred on what to do with criminals on probation. In May 2013, the Conservative and Liberal Democrat coalition government published a strategy paper called 'Transforming Rehabilitation', which set out to overhaul the probation system. Most radically, it proposed to privatize most parts of it, taking the oversight of medium- and low-risk offenders out of the public system and letting private enterprise take up the slack. The problem was framed as being one of reoffending. As the strategy made clear from the start, nearly half of people released from prison were going on to commit further crimes. For the government, this was a reflection of the lack of incentives in the public system to make sure criminals were rehabilitated properly.

The plan was, essentially, to *buy* better results. Contracts would be designed to reward the private providers that were actually successful at cutting reoffending rates. It would drive efficiency and innovation at the same time. It would embed a wraparound 'through the prison gate' set of supports to help offenders turn their lives around whilst keeping the public safer. It sounded almost too good to be true (and for good reason, as we'll come to shortly).

At first sight, this all seemed very much in alignment with the data and evidence – at least with those parts the government was keen to focus on. The statistics on rehabilitation and reoffending have never made for great reading. And numerous reports into the Probation Service confirm that it was constantly under pressure, under-resourced and over-extended. As the 'Transforming Rehabilitation' report itself noted, there is nothing simple about rehabilitation: 'We know, for example, that 15% of prisoners report that they were homeless before entering prison, and around a quarter are thought to suffer from anxiety and depression. Unemployment and substance misuse rates are also high amongst offenders.'[14]

The interventions to fix this formed a broad package, under-pinned by a market-based approach focused on procurement architecture that could essentially purchase better results. The principle is certainly logical, and governments across the world have become interested in variations on this theme through something called 'Social Impact Bonds' (SIBs). SIBs work kind of like a no-win, no-fee lawyer. Firms bid for government money by promising to deliver a particular social impact, and only get paid if they get the results promised. As ever, the problem is that strange incentives can kick in. Just like a no-win, no-fee lawyer might be wary of taking on hard cases with a lower chance of success, so too can these models see providers focus their energies on the people who are the easiest to help. It ensures they get paid, rather than potentially 'wasting' their efforts on the people with the most complex range of interrelated problems.

But in 2013 in the UK, the government had a clear policy proposal which seemed to have its ducks in a row. An appar-ently straightforward problem – i.e. reoffending rates being too high (although the reasons are multifarious, as already noted); well aligned with the data and evidence showing the extent of the issue, combined with a politically saleable narrative about the need to improve outcomes for both offenders and the community, which was itself aligned with clear policy interventions specifying what the government was actually proposing to do. That looked like a recipe for success.

It sure didn't end up that way. What the four ducks can't do is save governments from policy innovations that are just a fundamentally bad idea. Ideological clarity only gets you so far. Just ask those in the Thatcher government who had to wrestle with the extraordinarily unpopular poll tax in the late 1980s, which has become a byword in policy failure.

There are some things that are just particularly difficult to privatize. For example, the ministries of defence in most countries are often accused of not being efficient in the way they spend taxpayers' dollars. Dominic Cummings railed about this before and during his stay at Number 10 as Prime Minister Boris Johnson's chief adviser. There is a famous story in Australia of the Defence Department allegedly not being able to account for the whereabouts of all its tanks when asked by a parliamentary committee in 2005.[15] But few people would suggest that the answer to such problems is to privatize the army. It might be logical in economic terms – after all, mercenaries have existed for millennia. But that doesn't make it a good idea.

The criminal justice system is immensely complicated. It deals with some of the most fundamental aspects of our shared social existence: the safety of the community; the protection of victims; the rehabilitation of offenders. All this in an area in which people have drug and alcohol issues, and are facing joblessness, family breakdown, and more. This was literally too hard to 'solve' through the interventions the government wanted to try. There are some things the private sector is very good at. This is not one of them. The fourth duck was out of alignment.

We know that because these reforms were reversed after only five years in operation. There had been concern when the reforms were established in 2014, but it had come mainly from independent and academic commentators noting that the government was biting off an awfully hard morsel to chew.[16] As the next few years were to show, it was a meal that turned out to be pure gristle.

In some ways it could be written up as a failure of implementation (often a classic euphemism employed by politicians for passing the blame on to their civil servants). But multiple studies and sources demonstrate that the whole process should rather be seen as a 'case study in failure', as the London-based Institute for Government has dubbed it.[17] It was a poorly thought-through idea, based on a flawed outsourcing model, which failed to achieve its targets. In 2019, the chief inspector of Probation, Dame Glenys Stacey, provided a damning assessment in her annual report. She noted, for example, that probation was just not a good fit for this model of outsourcing: 'Experience has shown that it is incredibly difficult, if not impossible, to reduce the probation service to a set of contractual requirements and measures . . .'[18] Referring to it as an 'irredeemably flawed' model, the report showed that assessments by the inspectorate of the private providers of probation services had found their performance to be 'inadequate' on many key indicators.

Politicians tend to be much more practical and clear-headed

than their public rhetoric would necessarily suggest. Plenty of ministers and MPs in the government could see that this had been a bad idea that simply wasn't working. Reports such as that by the Inspector of Probation, combined with the political cover provided by the Covid pandemic, allowed for a clean change to bring probation services back 'in-house', where public providers could tackle problems directly. It is a reassuring sign in many ways that governments do take notice when things go awry. It would of course be preferable if things didn't go wrong in the first place.

Conclusion

Setting: *It has been a long and exhausting election campaign. With five days to go until election day, the prime minister is hanging on by a thread in opinion polls against a resurgent opposition. She is doing a live interview during the news bulletin of a key national television network. Her backdrop is the beautiful river city of Brisbane in the Australian state of Queensland, a key battleground state for the upcoming election.*

The prime minister's interlocutors are seated at their studio desk, a news-reading duo enjoying the chance to speak live with the PM.

Newsreader 1: 'Prime Minister, no mention today, or tonight as a matter of fact, about the carbon tax. Have you decided that's going to cost you votes, is that why it's on the shelf?'
Prime Minister: 'There will be no carbon tax under the government I lead . . .'

Politics is defined by moments. Thousands of small moments pass by each day without much consequence, and then suddenly a single sentence can become a part of history. The prime minister in this short scene was Australia's Julia Gillard. The year was 2010 and she was involved in a knife-edge election campaign in which climate change had become a central issue. She had taken up the mantle as prime minister only a few months before, when Kevin Rudd had spectacularly lost the support of his own party and been pushed aside. This election was Julia Gillard's big democratic test. Could she return the Labor Party to government in her own right as prime minister?

Election campaigns are much the same the world over. Thousands of words are spoken as leaders race across the country, flitting between photo opportunities and key election announcements. Whether it's Boris Johnson in a bulldozer, Donald Trump in a hard hat, or Julia Gillard silhouetted against the Brisbane River, the words and images keep flowing as they try to cut through with the electorate. So much of what is said is forgotten within a minute of it being uttered. Repeated phrases and mantras about strong leadership, a great country, and promises of fantastic successes to come. It's formulaic. Generic. Leaders try to avoid 'missteps', which means they try to avoid saying anything even slightly off the script they have been pursuing for weeks on end. To disillusioned citizens and journalists, it can sometimes all seem so pointless.

But we would be wrong to think it doesn't matter. Quite the opposite. A sentence uttered in haste can see leaders suddenly paint themselves into a corner through their own words. They set themselves rhetorical traps of their own devising and politics then does not let them out. It seems to happen particularly around the dreaded topic of tax. During almost every election, there seems to be one major party leader or presidential candidate who is pushed into saying something about tax that they then go on to regret. Just think back to President George H. W. Bush in the 1988 US presidential election campaign.

At the Republican National Convention, Bush stated emphatically: 'Read my lips: No new taxes'. Six words that would come back to haunt him. The reason politicians normally equivocate so much is because they know only too well that politics can force them into doing things they would rather avoid. For Bush, a Congress under Democrat control forced him to negotiate on various taxes, with some increases eventually being signed off. The deed was done. Opponents from both left and right never let Bush forget it. He lost the 1992 election and left office as a one-term president. As ever, there were many factors involved, but the tax pledge was undoubtedly a significant contributor to his fate.

In 2010, climate change was already a big political deal. The United Nations Climate Change Conference, held in Copenhagen in 2009, had seen world leaders make new pledges, even whilst overall agreement had remained elusive. Every politician on the planet had to have a view. The citizens certainly did. And in Australia, those citizens were increasingly inclined to be sceptical. Polling by the company Gallup showed that in 2008, 52 per cent of Australians agreed that global warming was caused by humans. By the election year in 2010, that had dropped to 44 per cent.[1] In 2008, 31 per cent saw it as a very serious threat, which had dropped to 22 per cent by 2010. The opposition Liberal/National Party coalition had been running hard on the economic damage that taking action on climate change would cause. Especially when Australia was not a leading global emitter in total output terms (although it definitely is in relative terms), why risk Australian jobs by insisting on something like a carbon tax?

It was a message that seemed to be cutting through. Right up to election eve in August 2010, opposition leader Tony Abbott continued to push the point: '. . . as surely as night follows day, if the government is re-elected . . . we will get a carbon tax. Whether it's a carbon tax as such or an emissions trading scheme, one way or another there will be a big, new slug on people's cost of living.'[2]

It was against this background that Julia Gillard had been questioned so specifically on that news bulletin just days before, leading her to rule out the introduction of a carbon tax. It was a fateful moment. That short declarative statement would follow her around like Banquo's ghost for years to come. The Gillard government retained office by a whisker, reduced to a minority by the 2010 election and left reliant on the supporting votes of the Greens Party (led at the time by Bob Brown in the Senate) and several key independents. A deal was struck with the Greens to bring in an emissions trading scheme, which would be shepherded into place by putting a price on carbon. It was all too easy for opponents to suggest that this was a carbon tax in all but name.

The response was visceral. One rally that has now become infamous took place in March 2011 outside Australia's Parliament House in Canberra. The protest was addressed by opposition leader Tony Abbott. In the background were plac-ards with slogans including 'Ju-liar – Bob Brown's Bitch', and 'Ditch the Witch'. It was ugly politics, laced with a degree of unprecedented personal vitriol directed against Australia's first woman prime minister. It was also a key stepping-off point that sparked a still ongoing discussion of misogyny in Australian politics.

In policy terms, the carbon tax debate provided a salutary lesson in how governments can get themselves stuck whilst ostensibly doing everything politically right. The government had met each of the four tests for getting its ducks in a row. There was by now a pretty clear problem definition around the issue of human-made climate change. Very few politicians in either major party still disputed it. There was a developing political narrative, a story to be told about the cost to future generations if no action was taken now. The data and evidence were already pretty overwhelming, with numerous authoritative scientific reports attesting to the realities of climate change and its effects. The intervention – an emissions trading scheme – was also fully in alignment with the other three aspects. Other countries had put such a scheme in place already, most notably the EU. The economic logic of providing incentives for companies not to pump carbon into the atmosphere was widely accepted. And even with increasing scepticism, a combined total of 69 per cent of Australians polled still thought that the consequences of climate change were at least 'somewhat serious'.[3] Why was this not simply a slam-dunk policy success?

What went wrong here was the politics. The government had painted itself into a corner during the election campaign, and no amount of wriggling enabled them to find the exit from their own rhetorical trap. In order to persuade voters to re-elect them, the prime minister had assured them that there would be no carbon tax. That promise is what then assured its downfall, much more than the merits of the actual policy itself. It's ironic, because there is surely little doubt that a price on carbon will become a necessity in the years ahead as urgent action against climate change ramps up. The ducks really were in a row. What they can't protect against is perceptions of political dishonesty, whether those perceptions are fair or not.

It's what Boris Johnson found out when he promised in the lead-up to Brexit that there would be no customs border in the Irish Sea. The reality suggests otherwise. Many people in Northern Ireland feel that a customs border is exactly what was put in place and have not been shy about saying so. It's what Nick Clegg found out when, as leader of the Liberal Democrats, he promised to oppose any increase in higher-education fees for students. When the coalition government in which he was deputy prime minister did the opposite by hiking those fees, the damage to trust in his party was immense. Voters were brutal in their punishment at the 2015 election, and even now their brand is still having to be rebuilt. The Conservatives, the lead partner in that coalition, suffered no comparable political pain. In fact, they were elected to a majority in their own right in 2015. For the Liberal Democrats, it wasn't the policy that destroyed them, but the broken promise.

Politics is a tough business. The fight for office is draining. Once elected, governing well is even tougher. There are so many factors that stop governments from getting the politics of policymaking right. When the disasters pile up, our leaders can very quickly look as though they have lost all control. Their intentions, however good, can simply be overwhelmed by perceptions that become just too hard to shift. There are no guaranteed paths to better outcomes. But what this book sets out is the sequence of actions that underpin success. Political and policy success comes from more than just spin. A good story alone is never enough. But nor is data and evidence sufficient. There also needs to be a well-defined problem with a well-targeted solution. Those four ducks need to get themselves in a row. It sounds easy. Experience would suggest it's not.

In many ways these four factors collectively represent what successful practitioners would think of as political instinct; a feel for the moment and what it requires. That starts with grasping the problem from the best available angle, seeing past the framing devices of others to realize where the heart of the issue resides.

It's about instinctively knowing that no matter how much students and parents might worry about potential grade inflation if exams aren't held, they'll worry a whole lot more about 'unfair' results being doled out by a robotic algorithm. Even if – in a purely technical sense – the algorithm would actually be more accurate, that does not make it palatable. It fails because it doesn't get to the core of the problem. And the nub of it all, in so many cases, is actually about how to reassure people that the government is genuinely doing the best it can. That it's trustworthy. That it cares. That it has your best interests at heart.

Take a problem like homelessness. It is multifaceted and complex. It has proved almost impossible for any government in the world to actually 'conquer' through public policy. Typically, much is left to charities and the NGO sector, supported by some government funding. Strategies come and go, promising changes which don't eventuate. Some pilot programmes in areas like social support, or drug rehabilitation, show successes, but then founder for lack of funding and investment. It's a classic wicked problem.

Yet, at the outset of the Covid pandemic, public health officials in the UK realized that something would have to be done. To maintain strict nationwide lockdowns capable of stopping the spread of the virus, homeless people would have to be supported to get off the streets. What's more, the cheek-by-jowl living arrangements in various hostels would not be sufficient to enable the kind of social distancing that would be required. What had for so long seemed an insoluble problem suddenly looked like a straightforward proposition: get homeless people into proper housing.

That view of the problem is, of course, not all that revolutionary. Worldwide, there have been many programmes in recent decades that have trialled what is called a 'housing first' approach. In other words, it simplifies the problem by suggesting that the first step in combating the interrelated difficulties of the homeless is to start by giving them a home, and worrying about the rest from there. It is a wonderful example of how to simplify problem definition down to core attributes that can then be dealt with through policy.

For the government, it was an easy sell as a policy narrative. What had previously been a problem overladen with centuries of moral judgements about the deserving and undeserving poor became at a stroke a public health issue instead. A crisis allowed for a crisis response. On the data and evidence side, homelessness is not really a hidden problem. Nobody who walks through a town square in any town in the UK is in any doubt that we have homeless people. Thanks to the extraordinary work of countless homeless charities, we have reasonable data on how many people are homeless and how they're distributed across the country. I say reasonable data; there remain many thousands of people that the system doesn't necessarily see.

Nonetheless, there was enough data to give the government what it needed. And the intervention was simplicity itself. Get a roof over people's head. It didn't much matter how or where. If it was in hotels, or B&Bs, or newly designated crisis accommodation, that was all fine. It didn't matter. Just bring them in.

Amongst the mayhem of much of the UK's early response to the pandemic outbreak, the determination to both protect the homeless and stop them becoming spreaders of the virus was a remarkable story. The 'Everyone In' strategy worked. It was successful in helping thousands get off the streets during the crucial months of the pandemic's first wave.[4] Funding and guidance was provided to local authorities to lead the measure.

Suddenly, this wicked problem which for so long seemed insoluble, was shown to actually be susceptible to the exertions of government after all (working in partnership with NGOs and local communities). A report by the Local Government Association concluded that the lesson for the future was: 'given the mandate and funding, councils, working with their partners, have the means to end the vast majority of rough sleeping'.[5] That's a pretty big call. And already, since those early successes, there are signs of backsliding as government funding begins to dry up and the country moves out of the crisis phase of the pandemic. But even critics acknowledge that swift action in those early weeks of March to May 2020 achieved impressive temporary results. It is a programme that undoubtedly saved lives. It also holds many useful lessons for governments who might be willing to dig deeper to combat longer-term homelessness.

The government had its ducks in a row on the issue. The problem definition, the message, the data and the intervention were all in alignment. But it also passed the wider test of political authenticity. There was no need for duplicity here, no spinning of subterranean agendas. The crisis had clarified things. The complexity had been sheered away and the issue reduced to its most basic form – the need to give people a roof over their head. It instinctively feels right. Which of us, if stopped by a pollster in the street and asked, 'What do you think the number one need of homeless people is?' would not answer: 'Well, a home would be a good start.'

The takeaway is that the often-substandard policy solutions we live with every day are not in fact inevitable. The homelessness example demonstrates that sometimes government just isn't trying hard enough in 'normal' times. Whether through providing the necessary money and resources, or a willingness to work through complexity and strip it back to what is actually at stake, extraordinary results are in fact possible.

It's not all about ducks. Sometimes the chickens also come home to roost. There are millions of families around the world keeping what we would think of as 'backyard poultry'. These are not commercial enterprises, or chicken farms, or anything of that nature. These are people who enjoy owning a few birds, which peck their way through the kitchen scraps and provide some eggs for the household. In good times, any surplus eggs might be given to the neighbours or sold for a bit of extra cash. It all sounds very wholesome. For the most part, that's exactly what it is.

But health authorities do retain concerns about cases of salmonella that originate from backyard chicken pens. It's not a huge problem, but that doesn't mean it isn't real. In the USA, the National Centers for Disease Control and Prevention monitor cases. In 2020, it noted 1,722 cases of human infection with salmonella originating from the keeping of backyard poultry.[6] Of those, 333 people ended up in hospital, and one person died. In a world so recently used to a daily deluge of shocking health statistics about Covid-19, those numbers may seem small. Nonetheless, there is clearly a public health risk. What should governments do?

Put yourself in the shoes of a political leader and work this through. The first thing to consider is whether this is something government should 'interfere' in at all. You know from the outset that there will be a sizeable community out there who will regard it as a form of nanny state overreach if the government starts messing with people's backyard chickens. But there are legitimate public health concerns that cannot necessarily be ignored. Some of the 2020 cases were part of seventeen different multi-state outbreaks. Imagine if one of those outbreaks actually got out of control. The damage could be extensive.

So, it starts with being clear about what the problem is. The problem is not actually chickens in people's backyards. The problem is the salmonella. You've got no issue with people keeping pet chickens if it doesn't lead to health concerns. It may seem like a small distinction, but it makes all the difference. Governments who are looking at the chickens rather than the salmonella are skewing the view from the outset.

The data and evidence are pretty clear, thanks to the work of the CDC and their counterparts across the world. Most developed, democratic countries are surprisingly good at tracking established public health problems of this kind. What you may not know as much about is how many people are actually keeping chickens at home. If it isn't a requirement to register and license all animals, then that kind of information is hard to gather with certainty. Keep in mind too that not all citizens do 'the right thing' in registering, even if it is required. There could be many thousands of chickens out there that we just don't know about.

Having decided that you need to do something to stop the spread of salmonella, how might you tell that story – how do you get the narrative to align? Perhaps you would focus on the case of one of your residents who has recently been hospitalized with salmonella, which they contracted from their own chickens. Such stories were told to powerful effect throughout the Covid pandemic by people who had been hospitalized and survived, or by the grieving relatives of someone who had refused the Covid vaccine and then ended up dying from the virus.

If you can get all of that to line up – the problem, the facts, and the story – then your big challenge remains what to actually do about it. What's the best intervention here? That really depends on all sorts of things. Is there a way of preventing the spread of salmonella whilst still allowing people to keep chickens? Is it just a question of hygiene, or are there other factors to consider?

That's how the politics of policymaking works. Those are the questions governments are asking themselves. The challenge is that policy isn't happening in the coldly reflective world of some book by an academic, but in the real-time world of aggravated people, lobby groups, families who have kept chickens for generations, public health officials, and hospitals worried about whether they could cope with a major outbreak of salmonella. That is why politics is so hard; even local and apparently simple issues have complexity involved.

Just ask the Washington D.C. City Council. In April 2017, press reports emerged that the administration of Mayor Bowser was looking to ban the practice of keeping backyard chickens in D.C. The problems started early in that the administration failed to clearly articulate what problem it was targeting. Press reports discussed salmonella, but the narrative from the administration was vague, focusing on keeping people safe and healthy, without necessarily explaining the connection. The provision was included as part of wider budget discussions, but quickly emerged as a bit of a cause célèbre, drawing attention from both local and national media.

The data and evidence were not clear on whether a complete ban was actually necessary to beat the underlying issues. The lack of a clear problem, clear evidence, and a clear story on why things needed to change proved fatal. The ducks weren't in a row, so the chickens flew the coop. The proposed policy change was overwhelmed by the cumulative impact of these defects. The idea was widely condemned in council health committee discussions, following public unrest, a petition with hundreds of signatures, and a lack of support amongst council members. The administration was forced to pull the proposal, with the city administrator having to reassure residents that 'this is not a war on pets'.[7]

It's all too easy in hindsight to poke fun at the council and the predicament it got itself into, but the story is a microcosm of the wider arguments of this book. Policy success relies on politics. The city health authorities could actually argue quite legitimately that there were public health issues to be addressed. They got stuck because of their inability to align a clear problem with clear data and a clear narrative. The city administration simply failed to get its story straight, its facts sharp, and its policy right. Without those fundamentals in place, governments do not give themselves any kind of chance at success. And our public policy results are the poorer for it.

The four-ducks framework shows how governments at all levels can sometimes get it wrong. But governments are not the only organizations that struggle with this kind of alignment. The same lessons are often applicable in the private sector too. Think of large social media companies grappling with the challenges of harmful online content, for example. Too often, the narrative which promises that the problem is being addressed doesn't match with the evidence. The ducks aren't in a row.

Even at a micro-level, the same rules apply. How many family arguments around the dinner table have at their source a misalignment between the problem, the evidence, the story and the intervention? Let's say you want to move house to downsize. Why – what is actually the problem? Is it that you have too many empty rooms to clean, or is it because your knees aren't coping well with the stairs? If it's the latter, then buying a small, three-storey cottage on the Devon coast doesn't make a lot of sense, even if you have fallen in love with it! Three stories mean too many stairs. The ducks aren't in a row. The problem doesn't match the evidence or the proposed solution.

At least around the kitchen table you have the chance to debate such things at length. The challenge for governments is that they are answerable to a democratic electorate in a way that private organizations and family units are not. They do not have the ability to slowly ride out their mistakes. For our politicians, the stakes are higher because the people on the receiving end of their decisions can vote them out of office. Time is not on their side, and the consequences of getting the ducks out of line are so much greater. But that doesn't mean it can't be done. The political and policy rewards will flow if things are handled right. It's time to get those ducks in a row.

Notes

Introduction – The Four Ducks

1   See Jaakko Kauko, 'The Finnish Comprehensive School: Conflicts, Compromises and Institutional Robustness', in Mallory E. Compton and Paul 't Hart (eds.), *Great Policy Successes* (Oxford: Oxford University Press, 2019), 122–42.

2   Notes on Type 2 Diabetes. Centers for Disease Control and Prevention. https://www.cdc.gov/diabetes/basics/type2.html

3   'Diabetes in India', posted 15 January 2019. https://www.diabetes.co.uk/global-diabetes/diabetes-in-india.html

4   Notes on the IDF Africa Region – South Africa. https://idf.org/our-network/regions-members/africa/members/25-south-africa.html

5   Speech by Senator Barack Obama on topic of 'Healthcare and Health Issues', delivered 25 January 2007. http://obamaspeeches.com/097-The-Time-Has-Come-for-Universal-Health-Care-Obama-Speech.htm

6   Speech by Senator John McCain, delivered 3 June 2008. https://www.politico.com/story/2008/06/transcript-of-mccain-speech-010820

7   'Remarks by the President to the Annual Conference of the American Medical Association', delivered 15 June 2009. https://obamawhitehouse.archives.gov/the-press-office/remarks-president-annual-conference-american-medical-association

8   Press release from CDC News Room, 'Nearly 44 Million in United

States Without Health Insurance in 2008'. Released 1 July 2009. https://www.cdc.gov/media/pressrel/2009/r090701.htm

9 Transcript of 'Obama's Health Care Speech to Congress', *New York Times*, 9 September 2009. https://www.nytimes.com/2009/09/10/us/politics/10obama.text.html

10 Liz Neporent, 'Obamacare Explained (Like You're An Idiot)', ABC News. Published 23 December 2013. https://abcnews.go.com/Health/obamacare-explained-idiot/story?id=21292932

11 *New York Times*, 'Obamacare Turns 10. Here's a Look at What Works and What Doesn't'. Published 23 March 2020. https://www.nytimes.com/2020/03/23/health/obamacare-aca-coverage-cost-history.html

1. Problems, Problems, Problems

1 John Swaine, 'We'll Scrub Banksy's Art, Insists New York Mayor', *Daily Telegraph*, 19 October 2013, 7.

2 'Speech from the Throne', delivered by His Excellency the Right Honourable David Johnston, Governor General of Canada. Delivered 4 December 2015. https://www.canada.ca/en/privy-council/campaigns/speech-throne/speech-throne.html

3 CBC News, 'Support for Electoral Reform Spikes after Federal Election, New Poll Suggests'. Posted 23 November 2019. https://www.cbc.ca/news/canada/british-columbia/support-for-electoral-reform-spikes-after-federal-election-1.5370921; Angus Reid Institute, 'Electoral Reform Revival? Support for Changing Voting Systems Skyrockets Post Election'. Posted 21 November 2019. https://angusreid.org/electoral-reform-trend/

4 Kelly Carmichael, 'Broken Trust on Electoral Reform', *Policy Options*. Posted 13 February 2017. https://policyoptions.irpp.org/magazines/february-2017/broken-trust-on-electoral-reform/

5 Ashley-Marie V. Hanna and Deborah M. Ortega, '*Salir Adelante* (perseverance): Lessons from the Mexican Immigrant Experience', *Journal of Social Work* 16/1 (2016): 47–65, at 55.

6   Michelle Ye Hee Lee, 'Donald Trump's False Comments Connecting Mexican Immigrants and Crime', *The Washington Post*. Published 8 July 2015. https://www.washingtonpost.com/news/fact-checker/wp/2015/07/08/donald-trumps-false-comments-connecting-mexican-immigrants-and-crime/

7   Kate Burke, 'Dilapidated Hoarder's House in Surry Hills Sells for $1.6 Million After Less Than a Week'. Posted 25 September 2017. https://www.domain.com.au/news/dilapidated-hoarders-house-in-surry-hills-sells-for-16-million-after-less-than-a-week-20170925-gyo1dj/

8   Michael Janda, 'House Prices Record Sharpest Increase Since 2003, CoreLogic says', ABC News. Posted 28 February 2021. https://www.abc.net.au/news/2021-03-01/house-prices-record-sharpest-increase-since-2003/13201992

9   Quoted in: Phillip Coorey and Jacob Greber, 'Scott Morrison Says High House Prices are "Real", Not an Investor Bubble', *Australian Financial Review*. Published 13 March 2017. https://www.afr.com/politics/scott-morrison-says-high-house-prices-are-real-not-an-investor-bubble-20170313-guwurn

10   Quoted in: Carrington Clarke, 'Labor's Negative Gearing Changes Will Force Property Prices Down and Rent Up, Study Says', ABC News. Posted 21 March 2019. https://www.abc.net.au/news/2019-03-21/property-prices-to-fall-under-labor-proposed-plans-study-says/10924650

11   Martin Farrer, 'Record Low Interest Rates Until 2024 Could Deepen Divisions Between Australia's Haves and Have-Nots', *The Guardian*. Published 2 March 2021. https://www.theguardian.com/australia-news/2021/mar/02/record-low-interest-rates-until-2024-could-deepen-divisions-between-australias-haves-and-have-nots

12   Speech by Anthony Richards, 'Some Observations on the Cost of Housing in Australia'. Delivered at the Melbourne Institute, 27 March 2008. https://www.rba.gov.au/publications/bulletin/2008/apr/pdf/bu-0408-5.pdf

13   Quoted in: Carol Rääbus, 'Experts Say This Is What Australia

Needs to do to Solve the Housing Crisis'. ABC News. Posted 26 February 2021. https://www.abc.net.au/news/2021-02-27/policy-ideas-to-solve-national-housing-crisis-australia/13185064

14 Dana Thomas, 'Why Won't We Learn from the Survivors of the Rana Plaza Disaster?' *New York Times*. Published 24 April 2018. https://www.nytimes.com/2018/04/24/style/survivors-of-rana-plaza-disaster.html

15 For an insightful recent study of the tragedy, see Gill Kernick, *Catastrophe and Systemic Change: Learning from the Grenfell Tower Fire and Other Disasters* (London: London Publishing Partnership, 2021)

2. Tell Me a Story

1 Deborah Stone, *Policy Paradox: The Art of Political Decision Making* (New York: W.W. Norton and Co., 2012), 158.

2 BBC News, 'Gay Marriage: Commons Passes Cameron's Plan'. Posted 21 May 2013. https://www.bbc.co.uk/news/uk-politics-22605011

3 Justice Anthony Kennedy's ruling in *Obergefell v. Hodges*, as transcribed in *Time Magazine*, 26 June 2015. https://time.com/3937983/supreme-court-gay-marriage-ruling-2/

4 Quoted in: Emma Griffiths, 'PM-elect Tony Abbott Tells People Smugglers "It's Over" Once He Takes Office', ABC News. Posted 10 September 2013. https://www.abc.net.au/news/2013-09-10/abbott-to-people-smugglers3a-27it27s-over27/4947924

5 Quoted in: Claire Phipps, 'Did Australia Pay People-Smugglers to Turn Back Asylum Seekers?', *The Guardian*. Published 17 June 2015. https://www.theguardian.com/world/2015/jun/17/did-australia-pay-people-smugglers-to-turn-back-boats

6 Quoted in: BBC News, 'Abbott: Australia's "Sick of Being Lectured" on Migration'. Posted on 9 March 2015. https://www.bbc.co.uk/news/world-australia-31792442

7 See Judi Atkins and Alan Finlayson, '"…A 40-Year-Old Black Man Made the Point to Me": Everyday Knowledge and the Performance

of Leadership in Contemporary British Politics', *Political Studies*, 61 (2012), 161–77.

8 J. Charteris Black, *Politicians and Rhetoric: The Persuasive Power of Metaphor* (London: Palgrave Macmillan, 2011), 14.

9 As cited in Billy Holzberg, '"Wir Schaffen Das": Hope and Hospitality Beyond the Humanitarian Border', *Journal of Sociology*, 57/3 (2021): 743–59, at 746.

10 As cited in Holzberg, 'Wir Schaffen Das', 747.

3. Getting the Facts Straight

1 Bryce Stewart and Griffin Carpenter, 'What Would Brexit Really Mean for the UK's Fishing Industry?', *The Conversation*. Posted 24 March 2016. https://theconversation.com/what-would-brexit-really-mean-for-the-uks-fishing-industry-56312

2 OECD Economic Policy Paper, 'The Economic Consequences of Brexit: A Taxing Decision', OECD Publishing, April 2016. https://www.oecd.org/unitedkingdom/The-Economic-consequences-of-Brexit-27-april-2016.pdf

3 Interview quoted in: PBS News Hour, 'Leaving EU Without a Brexit Deal Could Cause Major Disruptions in UK'. Posted 17 August 2018. https://www.pbs.org/newshour/show/leaving-eu-without-a-brexit-deal-could-cause-major-disruptions-in-uk. The gentleman interviewed for the PBS piece was back in the media in early 2021 expressing his view that the fishing industry had been misled by Brexiteer promises. See Joe Middleton, 'Leave-Voting British Fisherman Speaks of Brexit Regrets on Danish TV', *The Independent*. Posted on 20 April 2021. https://www.independent.co.uk/news/uk/home-news/brexit-leave-british-fisherman-eu-b1834389.html

4 Joe Owen, Marcus Shepheard and Alex Stojanovic, 'Implementing Brexit: Customs', Institute for Government. September 2017. https://www.instituteforgovernment.org.uk/sites/default/files/publications/IfG_Brexit_customs_WEB.pdf

5   Herbert A. Simon, *Models of Man* (New York: John Wiley, 1957).

6   Emma Harrison, 'Covid at Christmas: "Chris Whitty is More Popular than Britney Spears"', BBC News. Posted 19 December 2020. https://www.bbc.co.uk/news/uk-55333205

7   Quoted in: Marta Paterlini, '"Closing Borders is Ridiculous": The Epidemiologist Behind Sweden's Controversial Coronavirus Strategy', *Nature* (21 April 2020). https://www.nature.com/articles/d41586-020-01098-x

8   Our World in Data, 'Coronavirus (Covid-19) Cases'. https://ourworldindata.org/covid-cases

9   Joe Hasell, 'Which Countries Have Protected Both Health and the Economy in the Pandemic?', Our World in Data. Posted 1 September 2020. https://ourworldindata.org/covid-health-economy

10 Johan Ahlander, 'Sweden Saw Lower 2020 Death Spike Than Much of Europe – Data', Reuters. Posted 24 March 2021. https://www.reuters.com/article/us-health-coronavirus-europe-mortality-idUSKBN2BG1R9

11 Rafaela Lindeberg, Charles Daly and Bloomberg, 'Public Confidence in Sweden's Controversial COVID-Response Architect "In a Downward Spiral"', Fortune. Published 17 December 2020. https://fortune.com/2020/12/17/public-confidence-sweden-anders-tegnell-coronavirus/

12 Ibid.

13 Adam Taylor, 'The Best Place to Ride out a Global Societal Collapse Is New Zealand, Study Finds', *The Washington Post*. Published 29 July 2021. https://www.washingtonpost.com/world/2021/07/29/new-zealand-collapse/

14 New Zealand Ministry of Health Media Release, 'Single Case of COVID-19 Confirmed in New Zealand'. Published 28 February 2020. https://www.health.govt.nz/news-media/media-releases/single-case-covid-19-confirmed-new-zealand

15 World Health Organization Covid figures for New Zealand: https://covid19.who.int/region/wpro/country/nz

16   The Associated Press, 'Brazilian Comedian's Covid-19 Death Unites Nation in Grief', BCB News. Posted 6 May 2021. https://www.nbcnews.com/news/latino/brazilian-comedians-covid-19-death-unites-nation-grief-rcna848

17   Reuters, 'Brazil to Give Covid-19 Booster Shots to Elderly and Vulnerable'. Posted 25 August 2021. https://www.reuters.com/world/americas/brazil-give-covid-19-booster-shots-elderly-vulnerable-2021-08-25/

18   Alfredo Saad Filho and Fernanda Feil, 'Covid-19 in Brazil: How Jair Bolsonaro Created a Calamity', *The Conversation*. Published 23 April 2021. https://theconversation.com/covid-19-in-brazil-how-jair-bolsonaro-created-a-calamity-159066

19   Quoted in: Antonia Noori Farzan and Miriam Berger, 'Bolsonaro Says Brazilians Must Not Be "Sissies" about Coronavirus, As "All of Us Are Going to Die One Day"', *The Washington Post*. Published 11 November 2020. https://www.washingtonpost.com/world/2020/11/11/bolsonaro-coronavirus-brazil-quotes/

20   Quoted in: Tony Kirby, 'Canada Accused of Hypocrisy Over Asbestos Exports', *The Lancet*. Published 9 December 2010. https://www.thelancet.com/journals/lancet/article/PIIS0140-6736(10)62242-8/fulltext

21   Quoted in: Laura Payton, 'Canada Wins Battle to Keep Asbestos off Hazardous List', CBC News. Posted 24 June 2011. https://www.cbc.ca/news/politics/canada-wins-battle-to-keep-asbestos-off-hazardous-list-1.1124476

22   Kathleen Ruff, 'Exporting Harm: How Canada Markets Asbestos to the Developing World' (Ottawa, Ont.: Rideau Institute, 2009). https://rideauinstitute.ca/2008/10/30/exporting-harm-how-canada-markets-asbestos-to-the-developing-world/

23   Lorcan Archer, 'The Town Fighting Its Killer Reputation', BBC Worklife. Published 30 May 2018. https://www.bbc.com/worklife/article/20180529-the-town-fighting-its-killer-reputation

4. What Should We Do?

1   David G. Blanchflower, 'Is Happiness U-Shaped Everywhere? Age and Subjective Well-Being in 132 Countries', Working Paper 26641 (2020), National Bureau of Economic Research. https://www.nber.org/papers/w26641

2   See John W. Kingdon, *Agendas, Alternatives and Public Policies* (Boston: Little, Brown & Co, 1984).

3   'President Obama Speaks on the Shooting in Connecticut', White House Briefing Room. Posted 14 December 2012. https://obamawhitehouse.archives.gov/blog/2012/12/14/president-obama-speaks-shooting-connecticut

4   Quoted in: Carol D. Leonnig, Beth Reinhard and Tom Hamburger, 'Newtown Massacre Divided NRA Leaders, Foreshadowing Split to Come', *The Washington Post*. Published 4 July 2019. https://www.washingtonpost.com/politics/newtown-massacre-divided-nra-leaders-foreshadowing-split-to-come/2019/07/03/40c45d82-9757-11e9-916d-9c61607d8190_story.html

5   Kevin H. Wozniak, 'Public Opinion About Gun Control Post Sandy-Hook', *Criminal Justice Policy Review* 28/3 (2017), 255–78.

6   Kevin H. Wozniak, 'American Public Opinion About Gun Control Remained Polarized and Politicized in the Wake of the Sandy Hook Mass Shooting', LSE Blog. Posted 28 May 2015. https://blogs.lse.ac.uk/usappblog/2015/05/28/american-public-opinion-about-gun-control-remained-polarized-and-politicized-in-the-wake-of-the-sandy-hook-mass-shooting/

7   Mimi Kirk, 'What Research Says About Arming Teachers', Bloomberg CityLab. Published 14 March 2018. https://www.bloomberg.com/news/articles/2018-03-14/the-problem-with-arming-teachers-according-to-research

8   Nick Evershed, 'Strict Firearm Laws Reduce Gun Deaths: Here's the Evidence', *The Guardian*. Published 19 March 2019. https://

www.theguardian.com/news/datablog/2019/mar/20/strict-firearm-laws-reduce-gun-deaths-heres-the-evidence

9   Julian Santaella-Tenorio et al., 'What Do We Know About the Association Between Firearm Legislation and Firearm-Related Injuries?', *Epidemiol. Rev.* 38/1 (2016), 140–157. https://pubmed. ncbi.nlm.nih.gov/26905895/

10 CPH Post Online, 'A Celebration of Ice-Cold Water'. Posted 28 October 2015. https://cphpost.dk/?p=11830

11 Special Eurobarometer 472. Fieldwork December 2017, published March 2018. https://europa.eu/eurobarometer/surveys/detail/2164

12 Martin Armstrong, 'Where Obesity Is Most and Least Prevalent in the EU'. Posted 21 November 2019. https://www.statista.com/ chart/20057/obesity-rates-eu/

13 Edward Tenner, 'Denmark's Fat Tax: Now That's Rich!', *The Atlantic*. Published 10 October 2011. https://www.theatlantic. com/international/archive/2011/10/denmarks-fat-tax-now-thats-rich/246158/

14 Robert H. Lustig, Laura A. Schmidt, and Claire D. Brindis, 'The Toxic Truth About Sugar', *Nature* 482 (2012), 27–9. https://www. nature.com/articles/482027a

15 Signild Vallgårda, Lotte Holm & Jorgen D. Jensen, 'The Danish Tax on Saturated Fat: Why it Did Not Survive', *European Journal of Clinical Nutrition* 69 (2015), 223–6, at 224.

16 Henrietta Jacobsen, 'Study: "Fat Tax" Made Denmark Healthier', *Euractiv*. Posted 25 April 2016. https://www.euractiv.com/section/ health-consumers/news/study-fat-tax-made-denmark-healthier/

17 Malene Bødker et al., 'The Rise and Fall of the World's First Fat Tax', *Health Policy* 119 (2015), 737–42.

18 Quoted in: Clemens Bomsdorf, 'Denmark Scraps Much-Maligned "Fat Tax" After a Year', *Wall Street Journal*. Published 11 November 2012. https://www.wsj.com/articles/ SB10001424127887323894704578113120622763136

19 These events are well covered in work by Peter Whiteford at

the Australian National University. See: Peter Whiteford, 'Debt by Design: The Anatomy of a Social Policy Fiasco – Or was it Something Worse?', *Australian Journal of Public Administration* 80 (2021), 340–60. And: https://theconversation.com/robodebt-was-a-fiasco-with-a-cost-we-have-yet-to-fully-appreciate-150169

20 Quoted in: Matthew Knott, '"Strong Welfare Cop": Scott Morrison's New Self-Proclaimed Title', *Sydney Morning Herald*. Published 22 January 2015. https://www.smh.com.au/politics/federal/strong-welfare-cop-scott-morrisons-new-selfproclaimed-title-20150122-12vkqw.html

21 Quoted in: Christopher Knaus, 'Christian Porter Defiant on Centrelink's "Robodebt" Flaws: "This is Not a Matter for Apology"', *The Guardian*. Published 22 June 2017. https://www.theguardian.com/australia-news/2017/jun/22/christian-porter-defiant-on-centrelinks-robodebt-flaws-this-is-not-a-matter-for-apology

5. Ducks in a Row:
What Success Looks Like

1 Derek R. Smith and Peter A. Leggat, 'The Historical Decline of Tobacco Smoking Among Australian Physicians, 1964–1997', *Tobacco Induced Diseases* 4/13 (2008). http://www.tobaccoinduceddiseases.org/The-historical-decline-of-tobacco-smoking-among-Australian-physicians-1964-1997,65944,0,2.html

2 Australian Institute of Health and Welfare – Tobacco Smoking Snapshot. Released 22 July 2021. https://www.aihw.gov.au/reports/australias-health/tobacco-smoking

3 Katherine T. Hirono and Katherine E. Smith, 'Australia's $40 Per Pack Cigarette Tax Plans: The Need to Consider Equity', *Tobacco Control* 27 (2018), 229–33. https://tobaccocontrol.bmj.com/content/27/2/229

4 Barry Neild, 'Margaret Thatcher's Death Greeted with Street Parties in Brixton and Glasgow', *The Guardian*. Published 8 April

2013. https://www.theguardian.com/politics/2013/apr/08/margaret-thatcher-death-party-brixton-glasgow

5 Hugo Young, 'Margaret Thatcher Left a Dark Legacy That Has Still Not Disappeared', *The Guardian*. Published 8 April 2013. https://www.theguardian.com/politics/2013/apr/08/margaret-thatcher-hugo-young

6 Iain Duncan Smith, 'Her Legacy Is a Better Country and a Safer World for My Girls, Margaret Thatcher 1925–2013', *Daily Telegraph*, 11 April 2013, p. 2. (Retrieved via Factiva database.)

7 Jeremy Heywood and Bob Kerslake, 'Margaret Thatcher: Our Kindly Boss, by Britain's Top Civil Servants', *Daily Telegraph*, 15 April 2013, 1. (Retrieved via Factiva database.)

8 Quoted in: Rajeev Syal, 'Pro-Margaret Thatcher Article by Two Senior Civil Servants Angers MPs', *The Guardian*. Published 18 April 2013. https://www.theguardian.com/politics/2013/apr/18/pro-thatcher-artcile-civil-servants-row

9 Tom Clark, 'Thatcher's Flagship Policies Draw Mixed Support at Her Death', *The Guardian*. Published 9 April 2013. https://www.theguardian.com/politics/2013/apr/09/thatcher-flagship-policies-guardian-icm-poll

10 Speech to the National Housebuilding Council, 12 December 1984. https://www.margaretthatcher.org/document/105815

11 'Price of Existing Housing in the United Kingdom from 1990 to 2020', Statista. https://www.statista.com/statistics/233023/price-of-existing-dwellings-in-uk/

12 Hansard, Volume 967. Debated on 17 May 1979. https://hansard.parliament.uk/Commons/1979-05-17/debates/f4824eb6-2536-4cc9-99db-36c748fe6620/HousingAndLocalGovernment?highligh t=heseltine#contribution-9f37af4e-369a-4feb-87df-c68204d55587

13 Chris Foye, David Clapham and Tommaso Gabrieli, 'Home-Ownership as a Social Norm and Positional Good: Subjective Wellbeing Evidence from Panel Data', *Urban Studies* 55/6 (2018), 1290–1312. https://doi.org/10.1177/0042098017695478

14 See for example a discussion on whether home ownership in the US undermines community cohesiveness as people look to guard their individual house value over all other factors. Brian J. McCabe, *No Place Like Home: Wealth, Community and the Politics of Homeownership* (Oxford: Oxford University Press, 2016).

15 See Alan Murie, *The Right to Buy? Selling Off Public and Social Housing* (Bristol: Policy Press Shorts, 2016).

16 Soutik Biswas, 'Why India's Sanitation Crisis Kills Women', BBC News. Published 30 May 2014. https://www.bbc.co.uk/news/world-asia-india-27635363

17 BBC News, 'India Launches Scheme to Monitor Toilet Use'. Posted 1 January 2015. https://www.bbc.co.uk/news/world-asia-india-30647504

18 'Text of PM's Speech at Red Fort'. Published 15 August 2014. https://www.narendramodi.in/text-of-pms-speech-at-red-fort-6464

19 Sophie Bader, 'Privacy Please: The Controversial Approach to Ending Open Defecation in India and Nepal', *World Policy Journal* 35/2 (2018): 118–23.

20 Patralekha Chatterjee, 'Modi's Health Reforms: Between Hope and Hype', *The Lancet* 394 (2019), 1495–8; Vidhi Doshi, 'Narendra Modi to Face Down Critics by Hailing Clean India Scheme a Success', *The Guardian*. Published 30 September 2019. https://www.theguardian.com/global-development/2019/sep/30/narendra-modi-to-face-down-critics-by-hailing-clean-india-scheme-a-success

21 BBC News, 'India: Two Held for Killing Children for "Defecating in the Open"'. Published 26 September 2019. https://www.bbc.co.uk/news/world-asia-india-49835830

22 BBC News, 'India's Toilets: Report Questions Claims that Rural Areas are Free from Open Defecation'. Published 27 November 2019. https://www.bbc.co.uk/news/world-asia-india-46400678

23 Guðmundur D. Haraldsson and Jack Kellam, 'Going Public:

Iceland's Journey to a Shorter Working Week'. Published June 2021. https://autonomy.work/portfolio/icelandsww/

24   Ibid., p. 7.

25   'Prime Minister's Address at Chatham House in London'. Government of Iceland. Published 3 December 2019. https://www. government.is/ministries/prime-ministers-office/prime-minister/ katrin-jakobsdottirs-speeches-and-articles/speeche/2019/12/03/ Prime-Minister-Address-Chatham-House-London/

26   Haraldsson and Kellam, 'Going Public', op. cit., p. 53.

27   Anthony Veal, 'The Success of Iceland's "Four-Day Week" Trial Has Been Greatly Overstated', *The Conversation*. Published 13 July 2021. https://theconversation.com/the-success-of-icelands-four-day-week-trial-has-been-greatly-overstated-164083

28   Ibid., and see also: Nicole Kobie, 'What Really Happened in Iceland's Four-Day Week Trial', *Wired*. Published 12 July 2021. https://www.wired.co.uk/article/iceland-four-day-work-week

29   Annie Nova, 'A 4-day Workweek is the Norm in Iceland. Could the Same Become True in the U.S.?', CNBC. Published 12 July 2021. https://www.cnbc.com/2021/07/12/a-4-day-workweek-is-the-norm-in-iceland-could-the-us-follow-.html

30   ABC News, 'Female Stars Demand BBC "Act Now" to Close Gender Pay Gap'. Posted 23 July 2017. https://www.abc.net.au/ news/2017-07-23/female-stars-demand-bbc-act-now-to-close-gender-pay-gap/8736144

31   Nadja Bergmann, Alexandra Scheele and Claudia Sorger, 'Variations of the Same? A Sectoral Analysis of the Gender Pay Gap in Germany and Austria', *Gender, Work, and Organisation* 26/5 (2018): 668–87; Jacqueline O'Reilly et al., 'Equal Pay as a Moving Target: International Perspectives on Forty Years of Addressing the Gender Pay Gap', *Cambridge Journal of Economics* 39/2 (2015), 299–317.

32   Prime Minister's Press Release, 'My One Nation Government Will

Close the Gender Pay Gap'. Released 14 July 2015. https://www.gov.uk/government/news/prime-minister-my-one-nation-government-will-close-the-gender-pay-gap

33   David Cameron, 'Women's Raw Deal on Pay Has to End Now', *The Times*, 14 July 2015. (Retrieved via Factiva database.)

6. When the Ducks Don't Swim, Look Harder

1   Krystal Chia, 'Outback Town that Rivalled Manhattan's Prices Now Gathers Dust', Bloomberg. Published 7 June 2019. https://www.bloomberg.com/news/features/2019-06-07/australia-s-port-hedland-mining-boom-town-now-gathers-dust

2   Office for National Statistics, 'The 2008 Recession 10 Years On'. Published 30 April 2018. https://www.ons.gov.uk/economy/grossdomesticproductgdp/articles/the2008recession10yearson/2018-04-30

3   The Treasury, 'The Australia's Future Tax System Review: Timeline'. https://treasury.gov.au/review/the-australias-future-tax-system-review/timeline

4   Roy Morgan, 'West Australians Strongly Against Rudd's Proposed Mining "Super Profits" Tax'. Published 31 May 2010. http://www.roymorgan.com/findings/finding-4504-201302250359

5   'Kevin Rudd's Polling Since 2006', *Australian Financial Review*. Published 24 June 2010. https://www.afr.com/politics/kevin-rudds-polling-since-2006-20100624-ivajn

6   Ibid.

7   Quoted in: Emma Rodgers, 'Gillard Seals Mining Tax Deal', ABC News. Posted 1 July 2010. https://www.abc.net.au/news/2010-07-02/gillard-seals-mining-tax-deal/889138

8   Dolly R. Z. Theis and Martin White, 'Is Obesity Policy in England Fit for Purpose? Analysis of Government Strategies and Policies, 1992–2020', *Millbank Quarterly* (19 January 2021). https://doi.

org/10.1111/1468-0009.12498. https://onlinelibrary.wiley.com/doi/10.1111/1468-0009.12498

9   Quoted in: James Tapsfield, '"I don't want extra taxes on hard working people": Boris Johnson slaps down his eating tsar's "nanny state" call for new tax on sugary and salty food amid fury at the "madcap" £240 per family plan telling Brits they should be eating ALGAE instead of meat', Daily Mail. Published 16 July 2021. https://www.dailymail.co.uk/news/article-9790837/Fury-nanny-state-meddling-call-tax-sugary-salty-food.html

10 Steffanie A. Strathdee, Sally C. Davies, Jasmine R. Marcelin (2020) 'Confronting Antimicrobial Resistance Beyond the COVID-19 Pandemic and the 2020 US Election', *The Lancet* 396 (2020), 1050–3. https://www.thelancet.com/pdfs/journals/lancet/PIIS0140-6736(20)32063-8.pdf

11 'Antibiotic Resistance Threats in the United States 2019', CDC Report, Published 2019. https://www.cdc.gov/drugresistance/biggest-threats.html

12 Ibid., p. 13.

13 'Anti-Microbial Resistance: Tackling a Crisis for the Health and Wealth of Nations', The Review on Antimicrobial Resistance, chaired by Jim O'Neill. Published December 2014. https://amr-review.org/sites/default/files/AMR%20Review%20Paper%20-%20Tackling%20a%20crisis%20for%20the%20health%20and%20wealth%20of%20nations_1.pdf

14 Ministry of Justice (2013). *Transforming Rehabilitation: A Strategy for Reform*, p. 6. https://consult.justice.gov.uk/digital-communications/transforming-rehabilitation/results/transforming-rehabilitation-response.pdf

15 Louise Yaxley, '"Sensitive" Defence Gear Missing, Senators Told', ABC News. Posted 24 May 2005. https://www.abc.net.au/news/2005-05-25/sensitive-defence-gear-missing-senators-told/1577990

16 See Carol Hedderman and Alex Murphy, 'Bad News for Probation? Analysing the Newspaper Coverage of Transforming Rehabilitation', *Probation Journal* 62/3 (2015): 217–33.

17 Tom Sasse, 'Probation Outsourcing is a Case Study in Failure', Institute for Government. Posted 16 May 2019. https://www. instituteforgovernment.org.uk/blog/probation-outsourcing-case-study-failure

18 'Report of the Chief Inspector of Probation'. Published March 2019, p. 17. https://www.justiceinspectorates.gov.uk/hmiprobation/ inspections/report-of-the-chief-inspector-of-probation/

Conclusion

1 Anita Pugliese and Linda Lyons, 'Australians' Views Shift on Climate Change', Gallup. Posted 6 August 2010. https://news.gallup.com/ poll/141782/australians-views-shift-climate-change.aspx

2 Transcript of the Hon. Tony Abbott MHR Interview with Warren Moore, Radio 2GB Sydney, 20 August 2010. https://parlinfo.aph. gov.au/parlInfo/search/display/display.w3p;query=Id:%22media/ pressrel/NVQX6%22

3 Pugliese and Lyons, 'Australians' Views Shift', op. cit.

4 Ministry of Housing, Communities and Local Government, 'Dame Louise Casey's Statement on Coronavirus (COVID 19)'. Published 31 May 2020. https://www.gov.uk/government/speeches/dame-louise-caseys-statement-on-coronavirus-covid-19-31-may-2020; Patrick Butler and Peter Walker, 'Call to Provide Shelter for Rough Sleepers over UK Winter Lockdown', *The Guardian*. Published 7 January 2021. https://www.theguardian.com/society/2021/ jan/07/call-to-provide-shelter-for-rough-sleepers-over-uk-winter-lockdown

5 Local Government Association, 'Lessons Learnt from Councils' Response to Rough Sleeping during the COVID-19 Pandemic'. Published 19 November 2020. https://www.local.gov.uk/ publications/lessons-learnt-councils-response-rough-sleeping-during-covid-19-pandemic

6 CDC, 'Outbreaks of *Salmonella* Infections Linked to Backyard

Poultry'. Posted 17 December 2020. https://www.cdc.gov/salmonella/backyardpoultry-05-20/index.html

7   Peter Jamison, '"This is Not a War on Pets": D.C. Mayor Backs Off Proposed Chicken Ban', *The Washington Post*. Published 11 May 2017. https://www.washingtonpost.com/local/dc-politics/this-is-not-a-war-on-pets-dc-mayor-backs-off-proposed-chicken-ban/2017/05/11/390fc6f2-3684-11e7-b412-62beef8121f7_story.html

Acknowledgements

To write a book is to fumble in the darkness. You keep running into walls and tripping over furniture as you search for some kind of light source. I've been incredibly lucky to have a collection of supporters willing to help. My editor at Pan Macmillan, Matthew Cole, and my agent, Andrew Gordon, have been tremendous guides and sounding-boards. The publishing team have been extraordinary – patient, thoughtful and professional. My colleagues at Cambridge (both in POLIS and at Girton) have been greatly encouraging, and the Bennett Institute for Public Policy has provided a very nurturing intellectual home.

I'd like to thank my students, who continue to teach me so much about public policy. In particular, the students on the Cambridge MPhil in Public Policy (MPP), who each year burst into my life and share their enthusiasm, insights and expertise in a way that is quite infectious. Many of the examples I discuss in the book owe much to the students who first brought them to my attention. My faculty teaching colleagues on the MPP are some of the most amazing people I know. I'm a better academic, and quite possibly a better person, just for being in their company.

I retain adjunct affiliations at both Griffith University and the University of Tasmania, and am grateful to have such encouraging friends in both institutions. My thanks too must go to the many former colleagues I had the pleasure to work with in the Tasmanian Government, and earlier in the Australian Public Service. So much of what I know about politics and public policy I learned from working alongside people who care deeply about government being a powerful force for good in our societies.

To my mum and dad, friends and family, I'm grateful. Thank you for everything that you do. And especially to Kathy, who has listened patiently to the constant moaning that passes for my creative process.

Index